THE PLEASURES OF COOKERY

The Author

Frances Bissell has been described as one
of the best private cooks in Britain. Her
first book, *A Cook's Calendar*, was widely
acclaimed and called 'the book which
most accurately reflects the best cookery
of today'. She contributes to various
newspapers and magazines including
The Sunday Times and writes regularly for
A La Carte and *Homes & Gardens*. She lives
in north London with her husband Tom,
works for the British Council and is a
member of the committee of the Guild of
Food Writers.

The pleasures of cookery

FRANCES BISSELL

Dorling Kindersley

LONDON

A Jill Norman Book

First published in hardback in 1986
by Chatto & Windus Ltd, 40 William IV Street, London WC2N 4DF

First published in paperback in 1988
by Dorling Kindersley Limited,
9 Henrietta Street, London WC2E 8PS

British Library Cataloguing in Publication Data
Bissell, Frances
    The pleasures of cookery.
    1. Cookery, International
    I. Title
    641.5   TX725.A1
    ISBN 0—86318—267—4

Printed in Great Britain by
Redwood Burn Ltd,
Trowbridge, Wiltshire

FOR JANE GRIGSON

Contents

ACKNOWLEDGEMENTS

So many people over the years have had a part in my development as a cook that it would be impossible to thank them all by name. I am, nonetheless, deeply grateful to them.

A small band of people deserves my special thanks. One of the greatest pleasures in my life is to cook with others, particularly in their own kitchens. Not only do I get to know my friends better that way, but I learn how to use different equipment, learn new dishes and hear about old family traditions. Working side by side in a kitchen brings out a particular kind of intimacy and warmth which seems to add an extra something to the dish or meal finally produced, and it is, at the same time, simply tremendous fun. So I thank you Margaret Andrews, Clare Kirkman, Paul Levy and Penny Marcus, John and June Day, Elise Andrews, Sue and Raymond Elston, Sheila Clark, Marion Maitlis, David and Ann Miller, John and Elizabeth Dillon, Barbara and Ron Rohm, Alistair and Em Sawday, Robert and Mary Maloney, Bettina and Neil Maloney and Edith Bissell who have all indulged me, opened their kitchens to me and taught me far more than perhaps they realise.

Tricia Kemsley has once more typed my manuscript and I am grateful to her for that.

Brenda Jones, my editor at *The Sunday Times Magazine*, taught me to write down recipes in the right order. I would like to thank her for that and for all her help and good advice.

Tom, my husband, continues to support and encourage me in every possible way and I am grateful for his help, so lovingly given. He is still the best shopper I know.

Publisher's note
and oven temperature chart

Imperial and metric measurements are given in these recipes. The metric equivalents vary somewhat; for instance, in some recipes 30 g is given as an approximate equivalent for 1 oz, while in others 25 g is preferred. This is a matter of taste. Use one or other set of measurements; do not mix the two.

It should be remembered that the American pint is 16 fl oz in comparison to the Imperial pint, used in both Britain and Australia, which is 20 fl oz. The British standard tablespoon which has been used in this book holds 17.7 ml, the American 14.2 ml, and the Australian 20 ml. A teaspoon holds approximately 5 ml in all three countries.

Oven temperature chart

°C	°F	Gas mark	
110	225	$\frac{1}{4}$	very slow
130	250	$\frac{1}{2}$	
140	275	1	slow
150	300	2	
170	325	3	
180	350	4	moderate
190	375	5	
200	400	6	moderately hot
220	425	7	hot
230	450	8	
240	475	9	very hot

Introduction

For more than fifteen years now I have spent a good deal of my time in the kitchen. This has been by choice, as I love cooking for the two of us and for our friends. It takes time, energy, imagination and money, but then so do most serious hobbies. I have kept a detailed record of this absorbing passion. Thick household diaries record all the meals I have cooked, and when I study them I am often reminded of the occasion surrounding a meal, whether it was an anniversary supper, a welcome-home dinner, a long, late lunch that started at 5 p.m. on a cold, dark, rainy Sunday, or simply a quiet dinner for the two of us at the end of a long, hard week. The occasions themselves were always enjoyable. But so too was the preparation, the endless discussions about what to cook, what wine to serve with what dish; the lengthy shopping expedition and its occasional frustrations; the changes of mind. And then the hours spent experimenting and cooking in a warm, welcoming kitchen. The recipes that I give here are the fruits of my experiments, some recent, some based on the dishes that have become favourites over the years.

It would be quite wrong to claim that my methods of cooking, recipes and ideas about food have all been arrived at single handedly. Influences and inspirations are many; some recognisable, some subconscious. By looking back at the records I have kept of my cooking and entertaining over the years I can recognise the trends, the fashionable dishes of the time, the new cooking methods, books I was probably reading at the time, the increasing availability of new or unusual produce, the places where we spent our holidays. For example, casseroles, soups and smoked mackerel pâté were favourites in the very early 1970s. And no wonder. These were dishes which, as an inexperienced cook, I could prepare in advance of a dinner party, and could have dealt with any catastrophe in the cooking long before guests were due. Dishes from Greek, Indian and other ethnic cookery also figure largely in my food diaries. Inspired by dishes eaten in local restaurants or cooked by friends, moussakas and curries would be served regularly. A particular favourite was lamb paprika. First served by a friend in whose house we and a number of other people lived and where each of us would put £5 in the kitty for the week's food, I learned to prepare it and would cook it in the lowest possible oven overnight. We benefited twice from this. Not only did we have a delicious warming casserole the next day, but the very cold flat we lived in became blissfully warm for that one day.

In 1976 Michel Guérard's *Cuisine Minceur* was published and his style of cooking certainly influenced what I was doing in the kitchen. But at the same time I was trying out the sort of dishes we had eaten the same year in the Grand Véfour in Paris – traditional, classical French food. And so a *soufflé aux grenouilles* might be cooked one day, chicken steamed over vegetables and herbs the next.

So-called diets have not been ignored either. Two weeks of inventive spinach and egg recipes, with the odd day of steak tartare. Papaya and pineapple, enough to almost require a mortgage.

The influence of *nouvelle cuisine* has been important in attitudes to food and cooking. The emphasis on fresh, prime quality ingredients, cooked in the most appropriate manner, and served in a way to stimulate the senses, has long been a part of my cooking. For those characteristics, and not for its excesses, we should remember and be grateful for the move towards *nouvelle cuisine*.

All the early influences on my cooking have been French, from the chef who earned more than the principal in the Ecole Normale d'Institutrices in Albi where I spent a year in 1968, through Elizabeth David's descriptions of French country and provincial food, Jane Grigson's accounts of going to the market in 'her' part of France, our own experiences of it, as it were, eating our way through the various guide books to France, talking to the chefs whose food we have enjoyed, to reading about what the chefs of today are doing in their kitchens. Among these must be counted Anton Mosimann whose *cuisine naturelle* is an exciting new development. A week after I had eaten some of his new dishes, I cooked a dinner party for six which included a saffron-flavoured, jellied terrine of sole with vegetables; salad with artichokes and grilled leg of wild duck; breast of wild duck with pomegranate sauce served with ceps and a celeriac purée, and a tropical fruit salad. The meal was cooked without butter, cream, sugar, salt, oil or alcohol and my guests did not notice until I described how I had cooked the various dishes. Whilst I do not pretend to eschew these ingredients entirely, it is true to say that I have adapted many of my own recipes so that less butter and sugar are used. Sometimes instead of using cream I will use a *fromage blanc* or yoghurt or *tofu* (soya bean curd). I am very interested in Anton Mosimann's use of this ingredient to enrich and thicken sauces. Some years ago we stayed with friends, one of whom was vegetarian and who had also spent three years in Japan. She used *tofu* a great deal in her cooking, as well as soya bean milk and soya bean flour. I remember using it once or twice at home after that, but not until now have I started using it regularly. It can be bought in health food, wholefood or oriental grocers and delicatessens.

I came late to Italian food, but I have to say that the style of food preparation in Italy has become an important part of my daily cooking. Large fresh salads, small portions of simply cooked fish or meat, a dish of pasta, followed by fresh fruit is a typical meal. We find this a delicious way of eating, and infinitely varied; different shapes, and therefore different textures, of pasta combined with sauces of every kind produce wonderfully appetising dishes. Some I cook from ideas gathered on travels in Italy; most I cook because I have a particular herb, vegetable or other ingredient available. I find that this way of eating is entirely in harmony with generally held views on what constitutes a balanced diet for every day. Now, in 1986, I find my cooking is a mixture of what has gone before. No particular style dominates. It is no longer French, or Italian, *nouvelle* or *naturelle*, vegetarian or wholefood. But all of those elements are here. The consistent thread throughout is, I think, my insistence on the freshest, most natural ingredients. And, too, a reduction in the quantity of meat I cook. Game is now much more readily available than it was ten years ago, and as farmed venison is to be had throughout much of the year, that will often be served where I once might have had lamb or beef. The soups, casseroles and root vegetable dishes I used to cook years ago now have their place in my cooking once again alongside delicately arranged salads of unusual combinations. A dish of pasta might appear in the same meal as a small mousseline of red mullet sitting in its pool of vanilla sauce. A classic, rich dish of *Sole Grand Véfour* will appear, just occasionally, after a platter of herb-steamed vegetables. And why not? It's much more fun that way.

One of the original working titles of this book was 'Healthy Treats'. The more I developed the recipes and thought about food in a fairly concentrated way, the less happy I became about the title. It was too simple, dangerously full of pitfalls. What is healthy food? And does the same healthy food have the same good effect on all who eat it? I am not a nutritionist, but even turning to the specialist we receive equivocal answers on many of the current food issues. Take the butter versus margarine debate. Butter is a natural food but it is pure dairy fat, saturated fat which can harm those likely to suffer from heart disease and increase cholesterol levels. Sunflower margarine is made from a natural product originally but may have had much done to it, particularly in the way of additives, colouring and stabilisers before it reaches us on the supermarket shelves. On the other hand, it is based on unsaturated fats and is low in cholesterol. It will be healthier for someone allergic to additives to eat butter; for those concerned about their cholesterol levels, one of the margarines low in unsaturated fats would be best. Those watching their weight should avoid large quantities of either. But which is the 'healthy' food?

Fibre, we are told and most of us accept, is essential for a healthy diet. For years we carefully sprinkled wheat bran on cereal, baked with wholemeal flour and generally put bran back into products from which it had been removed. Wheat bran, we then learned, was an insoluble fibre and could be an irritant. What we should have been eating was soluble fibre. Beans and tomatoes, for example, and porridge for breakfast.

The debate shifts, the various protagonists regroup, but what is in it for me, the consumer, the cook? Information. Gradually, slowly, producers and growers are telling me what is in the food I eat and cook. The choice then lies fairly with me. I am in a position to decide what is best for me and the people I am cooking for.

Of course, the debate is slightly less pressing and I am in less of a quandary if I stick, as I do, to fresh food, food to be made into deliciously edible dishes with no hidden, unnecessary ingredients. I can judge how much sugar I want or need to sweeten a sponge cake. It is up to me to decide whether to use butter, oil, margarine or a non-stick pan in which to fry a piece of fish, thus controlling the amount of fat in the dish. In making a casserole I am the one who judges how much, if any, salt goes into it and, heaven forbid, any sugar. If a dish I have devised calls for wine or spirit, it will do so for a reason, for the particular character and flavour it adds to the end product through the initial marinating or the final spirituous dash to the sauce. If a sauce needs enriching I, not some faceless manufacturer, will decide how to do it. And I will do it by first examining the dish itself – what are its constituent parts? Will a cream or purée enrich it best? Then I will look at the dish in relation to the rest of the meal. What, if it is a main course, precedes it? What follows? A milky pudding following a creamy sauce would be unappealing to the eye, the palate, or the digestion.

I hope that those who read and use this book will also make similar judgements where they feel it suits their particular needs. My recipes are adaptable. Wines can be added to or removed from marinades. Oil can be used instead of butter for cooking fish or vegetables, and vice versa. Flour mixtures can be changed. Cream can be substituted for yoghurt or *tofu*. Such variations will change the final dish, in texture perhaps, or flavour; in nutritive value, calorific or fibre content. But the end product will be as good as the original recipe. The only area in which the cook cannot compromise is in the quality of the ingredients used. These must be the freshest, finest you can find and afford. Best does not mean dearest. The recipe for mackerel on p. 89 calls for one of the cheapest fish available, but it must be absolutely fresh. If you cannot get mackerel, try the recipe with whatever fish is available and fresh. The success of the carrot, fennel and apple soup on p. 27 depends on using firm, sweet-flavoured carrots – which means fresh carrots. Implicit in the list of ingredients for each of my recipes is the qualification 'good'. Editors do not like you to say '2 tablespoons good olive oil'. But that is what I mean. And not only good, but best. I mean extra virgin olive oil, which is clearly so described on the label. Its qualities are so superior to 'olive oil' or 'pure olive oil' or 'guaranteed pure olive oil' or other similarly described oils that you would do as well using a sunflower oil as any of the lesser olive oils. When I indicate that butter is required I mean the best, unsalted, freshest butter you can find. Why use salted butter, adding more salt to a dish than you might need? You should be the one to decide how much salt to add.

What I cook is determined to a very large extent by what is available when I go shopping. I might have it in the back of my mind that I want to prepare a dish of pasta with broccoli, but find that the broccoli is past its best or simply not around. But, since the spring onions look good, why not use those chopped up with some tomato and garlic for a light, fresh sauce? My recipe for venison with passion-fruit on p. 108 originally started life as an idea for venison marinated in pomegranate juice. The day I wanted to cook it, pomegranates were nowhere to be found, but a few wrinkled passion-fruit suggested another possibility. When I finally found pomegranates again, it was with wild duck that I first used them, and then with *noisettes* of lamb. Many of my recipes have been arrived at through what might have initially seemed a constraint, but turned out to be a stimulus to me to produce something new.

In this book, rather than give seasonal menus as I did in *A Cook's Calendar*, I have arranged the recipes in a more traditional form, working through the possible components of a meal. You might want to make up a vegetarian meal. All the components are here. Perhaps what you have in mind is a simple lunch. Here you will find soup recipes which can be combined with a salad and a light pudding. Many of the recipes and ideas can be adapted for you to prepare an array of cold or hot snacks. I have given notes on availability and suitability for different seasons where they seem to be called for, as well .as suggestions for substitutes. From this collection of recipes an almost infinite number of meals can be prepared, to meet many different occasions and tastes. The section in which you will find fewer recipes is the pudding section. For me, cooking is entirely personal and this reflects my own taste. I do not serve many puddings, but I hope that the ones I have given can be used as a base for your own experiments.

Soup

Vegetable soup was the first dish, and as it turned out, the only dish I was taught to cook in my first-form domestic science class. The end product could not be described as vegetable soup. It was truly awful. A carrot, an onion, a leek, a small turnip and a stick of celery were chopped into identically sized dice and set to boil in a very large pan of water until cooked soft. Salt and pepper were then added. I was to take it home in a thermos flask for the family's supper. Fortunately I come from a family who take soup very seriously and I quickly gave up cookery at school for needlework. It was also my good fortune that my mother is an accomplished needlewoman. Otherwise, today I should probably be inept in both skills.

I disagree with those who say that soup has no part to play in a formal meal and I serve it at dinner parties in summer and winter alike. A smooth, exquisitely coloured, delicately flavoured chilled soup, served in small glass bowls, is one of my favourite starters for a summer dinner party. It seems to go down well with guests too, and so I shall continue to serve it.

For everyday meals, either as a first or main course, soup can be given a more robust treatment by leaving the ingredients unsieved, as in the bean and minestrone soups and fish soups.

But whether you are making a simple, delicate soup or a robust, peasant dish, the ingredients must be of high quality. Soup is not an excuse to throw every possible leftover into the pot. If you do so, you will be left with a muddy coloured soup with no particular or distinctive flavour. The ideal base is a well-flavoured fresh stock, either meat, fish or vegetable stock. Stock can be made from carcasses of poultry or game or other meat bones, cooked or uncooked, fish scraps and pieces, and whole raw vegetables or vegetable trimmings. It should cook slowly, be carefully strained and then seasoned lightly.

Quite often I will make a larger pot of soup than is required for one meal and put the surplus in the refrigerator to make a different version of the soup the next day. For example, the minestrone soup on p. 71 might, the next day, become a supper dish of *zuppa alla frantoiana*, a Tuscan speciality. You make a purée of most of the soup and bring it to the boil, add it to the rest of the soup and pour it into hot soup bowls over a thickish slice of two or three day-old bread sprinkled with olive oil. It is heavenly on a cold night such as the one when I first tasted it in Lucca one January.

STOCKS

Home-made stocks are not the daunting task many people imagine them to be. A pot of chicken carcasses and vegetables can be left quite happily to simmer for a morning or an afternoon on the back of the stove. Or put the ingredients in an ovenproof deep dish, cover with a lid or foil, put them in the oven, use the timer switch and you have a pot of stock by the time you get home from work.

What can go into stock? Cooked or uncooked chicken, turkey, duck or game carcasses: meat bones, cooked or uncooked, although there will be little flavouring left in, say, a ham bone that has made its first appearance in a slow-cooking *cassoulet*. The peelings of vegetables that have first been scrubbed. Over-ripe tomatoes, stalks and all. Fish bones and trimmings, usually uncooked, but a quickly grilled sole will still have plenty of flavour and gelatine left in its bones if you put it in a little water with a piece of celery stalk, a twist of lemon or orange zest and a little onion.

Is there anything best left out of stock? This is often a matter of taste. For example, I am not too keen on the sweetish flavour given by adding the shells and heads of Greenland prawns to fish stock. I am also careful about adding herbs. Parsley and coriander stalks are fine, and a tarragon leaf or two, but when it comes to the oily, pungent herbs such as rosemary and thyme, I tend to leave these out, and only add them to a soup or sauce when required. Nor do I like to use cabbage or cauliflower trimmings in vegetable stock. Come to that, I'm not very fond of the brassicas in any shape or form. And cooked vegetables seem not to be a good idea. They add nothing but mush and make the stock cloudy. On the other hand, marinated vegetables that have sat in a winy bath to add their flavour to a piece of beef or a brace of wild duck also add plenty of flavour to a meat stock.

Whilst it is fairly obvious that fish stocks are needed for fish soups and game stock for game soups, it is not always appreciated that vegetable soups are best made with vegetable stocks. If you use chicken stock to make tomato, carrot or lettuce soup, for example, they will all have an underlying similarity of flavour which disguises the true flavour of the main ingredient.

Here are four basic stock recipes with suggested variations. The recipe for game broth on p. 30 describes how to make game stock. Fish and vegetable stock should be used within a day or two. Meat stock will keep for a few days but should be boiled up every two days for 5 minutes. In every case, stock should be cooled rapidly, covered and refrigerated.

Since a number of the recipes call for fish stock, here is my standard and very adaptable recipe, a base for sauces or soups. If, for example, you are buying sole, ask your fishmonger to fillet it and wrap the bones, head and skin separately, together with any other bones he can spare.

Fish stock
MAKES
1¾ pints/
1 litre

1 teaspoon olive or sunflower oil	Watercress, parsley, fennel etc. – as available
1 onion	1 or 2 squashy tomatoes
1 carrot	1½ lb/675 g fish bones and pieces
1 stick celery	
1 leek	1¾ pints/1 litre water

Use the oil simply to rub around a heavy saucepan, to stop bits sticking to it. Peel and chop or slice the vegetables and turn these in the pan until *just* beginning to turn colour. Chop the fish bones and pieces to fit your saucepan, add them to the pan and cook until opaque. Add the herbs. Pour on the water and bring slowly to the boil. Simmer gently, covered, for 40 minutes. Strain. Cool and refrigerate until required. Do not season at this stage since the stock will often need to be much reduced for a sauce, and salting at the stock-making stage will ruin the end result.

Whenever possible, try to make your stock well in advance and in a well-ventilated kitchen. Regrettably the smell of fish stock does linger. In the kitchen. In your hair. In your clothes.

Vegetable stock
MAKES
2 pints/
1.2 litres

1 medium onion	A few parsley stalks
2 carrots	2 or 3 ripe tomatoes
2 sticks celery including tops	2–2½ pints/1.2–1.5 litres water
1 leek	3 oz/75 g split lentils

Peel and slice or chop the first four vegetables. Brown them lightly in a non-stick pan. The sugar in the vegetables caramelises when it reaches a certain temperature and it is this browning which will colour the stock. It is important not to burn the vegetables. The stock will taste bitter and be too dark if that happens. Add the parsley stalks and the roughly chopped tomatoes, seeds and stalks included. Pour on the water and bring slowly to the boil. Skim the surface as necessary. When boiling, add the lentils. Bring back to the boil. Skim again and simmer gently for 1½–2 hours. Strain. Cool and refrigerate.

Chicken stock from a roast chicken carcass
MAKES
1½ pints/
900 ml

I usually pot roast my chickens and make the stock in the same pot, which is by then well flavoured with cooking juices and bits stuck to the bottom.

1 cooked chicken carcass	1 small onion
Any left-over gravy	1 carrot
2 pints/1.2 litres water	1 stick of celery
Parsley stalks	2 ripe tomatoes – optional
Small piece of orange or lemon zest	

Break up the carcass and put in a pan or casserole, together with any left-over cooking juices. Add water, the parsley stalks and the zest and bring slowly to the boil. While it is coming to the boil, peel and chop the vegetables and add these to the pot. When the liquid boils, skim it, reduce the heat and simmer, uncovered, for 1½ hours, by which time the stock will have reduced to about 1½ pints/900 ml.

The same basic method can be used for making stock from any cooked poultry or game bird carcass.

Shin bones make the best stock. Have the butcher saw them into manageable pieces.

*Simple beef
or veal stock*

MAKES
1½ pints/
900 ml

3 lb/1.3 kg veal knuckles or beef shin bones
1 piece pork skin or a few bacon rinds
1 medium onion
2 carrots
2 sticks celery
1 leek

1 small white turnip – optional
2 or 3 ripe tomatoes
Parsley stalks
A few sprigs watercress
Splash of white wine
A few peppercorns – optional

Place the bones in a sieve and pour a kettleful of boiling water over them to blanch them. Rinse them under cold water and put them in a large pan. Cover with water, about 2½–3 pints/1.5–1.8 litres and add the pork skin or bacon rinds. Place on a very low heat and bring to simmering point. Meanwhile peel and slice or chop the vegetables and add them to the pan, together with the parsley, watercress, wine (if you are using it) and peppercorns. When it comes to the boil, skim it thoroughly and simmer for 2½–3 hours. Remove the bones carefully and strain the stock through a fine sieve, lined with muslin if necessary, into a clean pan. Reduce to 1½ pints/900 ml over a steady heat. Cool. Cover and refrigerate. A particularly rich and gelatinous stock can be made by adding one or two pigs trotters instead of the pork skin. After 2 hours or so, they will be quite tender, can be cooled, rolled in breadcrumbs and melted butter and grilled to give you a delightful supper for two of *pieds de porc St Ménéhould.*

COLD SOUPS

Vegetable soups that have been cooked and then chilled are deliciously rich and smooth, but an uncooked vegetable soup has a wonderfully fresh flavour. The best known is perhaps the Andalusian *gazpacho*, full of tomatoes, bread, olive oil, garlic and other bits. I have also made a cold soup by putting the remains of a green salad in the blender with some stock and skimmed milk. Blended and then sieved, a remarkably elegant, pale (and tasty) green soup resulted.

Here are two recipes for when you have a glut of tomatoes and cucumbers in the greenhouse.

Tomato and orange soup
SERVES 4

1 lb/450 g ripe tomatoes
Juice of 4 freshly squeezed oranges
1⅓ pint/800 ml vegetable stock

Fresh basil, if you have it
Parsley
Salt and pepper

Roughly chop the tomatoes, top and all, which adds its own flavour. Put in the blender with the orange juice, stock, herbs and a little seasoning. Blend until smooth and then sieve, forcing through as much of the pulp as possible, which will leave only the seeds and skin to throw away. Check the flavour to see if any more seasoning is required. Serve immediately, with an ice cube or two floating in it to chill it quickly.

Cucumber and watercress soup
SERVES 4

1 cucumber
1 bunch watercress
½ pint/300 ml vegetable stock

½ pint/300 ml skimmed milk
2 cloves garlic – optional
Salt and pepper

Roughly chop the cucumber and place in the blender. Wash and pick over the watercress, removing any yellowing leaves. Add to the blender with the stock, milk, crushed garlic and a little seasoning. Blend until smooth. Sieve, season again and serve immediately.

Chilled carrot and tomato soup
SERVES 6

1 small onion
½ lb/225 g carrots
½ lb/225 g ripe tomatoes
2 pints/1.2 litres vegetable stock

Seasoning
1 tablespoon *tofu* or *fromage frais*
Chervil, parsley or watercress to garnish

This is best cooked in a non-stick saucepan in order to avoid any oily surface on the soup. Chop or thinly slice the onion. Peel and thinly slice the carrot. Roughly chop the tomatoes, leaving the stalks on. Cook the vegetables together with a little stock until soft. Allow to cool. Put in the blender, with the rest of the stock, in two batches. Process, with the *tofu* or *fromage frais*, until smooth. Season if necessary. Sieve and allow to cool completely before refrigerating until required.

1½ lb / 700 g courgettes
1 small onion
2 cloves garlic
1 tablespoon olive oil
2 pints (1.2 litres) stock

1 teaspoon cornflour
5 fl oz / 150 ml smatana
Salt and pepper
1 bunch dill – about
   2 tablespoons

Chilled
courgette
and dill soup
SERVES 8

Wash and slice the courgettes, trimming off the hard ends. Peel the onion and garlic and chop them finely. Heat the olive oil in a heavy based pan and stir in the vegetables. Pour on 5 fl oz / 150 ml stock and cook the vegetables until soft. Mix the cornflour with a little more stock and add it to the vegetables. Cook it until you can no longer taste the raw flour.

Allow to cool slightly. Stir in the smatana, season to taste and add half the dill which you should roughly chop first. Blend in batches, adding some of the rest of the stock to each batch. Pour into a decorative bowl and chill. Just before serving garnish with the rest of the dill and perhaps a little more smatana.

Almond soup
SERVES 4

Recipes are written down for all kinds of reasons. One writer, within the same book, even within the same piece, will have different motives for devising or recording different dishes. It may be a wish to pay homage to a great cook. It may be prompted by having seen an unusual item in the fish or vegetable market, or an unfamiliar ingredient on display in the local delicatessen – someone after all must have used the first pink peppercorn. It may be a wish to try out a new variation on a classic theme – hence chocolate ravioli with game.

However we are not always moved, all the time, by the spirit of adventure. Occasionally we want to look back. I use recipes as some people use photographs. When I taste something I like in a place I like or at an occasion that pleases me, I make notes on it so that I can reproduce it once back in my kitchen. Preparing it again months or years after the event, the time and place are precisely evoked. Proust's was an accidental experience. Mine is quite deliberate.

Few dishes illustrate this point quite as explicitly as *gazpacho blanco*, a delicious chilled almond soup I first tasted in Cordoba. Before that I had thought there was only one *gazpacho* – the tomato and olive oil based *gazpacho andaluz*. In fact there are three – the two already mentioned and a bean *gazpacho*.

But to the *gazpacho blanco* or *almendro*. Not only does it taste as if it comes from a particular place, it looks as if it comes from a particular place. The narrow streets of Cordoba near the Mezquita, the towns of Montoro or Baena seen from a distance; white-washed walls, small dark square windows: perhaps it is fanciful to say that these elements are reflected in the *gazpacho blanco* but, to me, those are the scenes it recalls when I look at it in all its paleness, studded with dark raisins. And when I taste the smooth nuts and rich fruit the scene is enhanced in my mind by almond trees in blossom, by acres and acres of vineyards nursing the next harvest of Moriles. Reflecting on the past of that part of Spain, I realise that this soup must come directly from Spain's Moorish era. Thus the dish has far more than an appeal to the palate; it is curiously satisfying in its completeness.

This is how I made it after tasting it once in El Churrasco at Romero 16, Cordoba. You can use chicken or vegetable stock.

4 heaped tablespoons ground almonds	2 teaspoons best olive oil
½ pint/300 ml water	Seasoning
¾ pint/400 ml stock	Garlic
	Raisins, apples, *croûtons*

Place the ground almonds in a jug. Pour on sufficient *boiling* water to cover well, about ½ pint/300 ml should do. Of course, freshly picked and shelled almonds which you pound yourself would have far more flavour. Even whole almonds bought in packets, blanched, peeled and pounded, would be better. If you can only find ready ground almonds, add a pinch of sugar to each tablespoonful which helps to bring out the flavour.

By the time the liquid has cooled, the almonds will be sufficiently steeped for you to proceed. Stir in the stock, 2 scant teaspoons of best olive oil, salt and white pepper to taste. Finely crush two or three cloves of freshest garlic and stir this in. Chill. Serve in earthenware bowls and hand the garnish round separately – finely diced apples, raisins and small *croûtons*.

Sharp, sweet, fragrant and unusual, this is a dish which really awakens the tastebuds. You can use chicken, veal or vegetable stock as the base, since the fennel has such a distinctive flavour.

Chilled apple and fennel soup
SERVES 4

1 small onion or 2 shallots
1 medium sized fennel bulb
2 or 3 apples
1⅓ pint/800 ml strong stock

1 tablespoon Greek yoghurt
Chives and chive flowers
Seasoning

Peel and slice the onions, fennel and apples. Cook them very gently in a non-stick saucepan until soft together with a quarter of the stock. Allow to cool then put in the blender with the rest of the stock and the yoghurt. Reserve a few lengths of chives and the chive flowers for garnish and snip the rest into the blender. Blend until smooth and then sieve to give a fine, smooth cream soup. Unsieved it will be rather fibrous, though still delicious. Chill the soup and, to serve, garnish each bowl with two or three chive flowers and lengths of chives.

This is a fresh, simple soup for summer, to be served hot or cold. The lettuce gives it a clean, bright colour, the courgettes give it body. It makes a good starter to a vegetarian meal, as do any of the vegetable stock based soups. By using a non-stick pan to cook the onions, you can completely cut out any oil or butter.

Lettuce and courgette soup
SERVES 4

1 medium onion
1 lb/450 g courgettes
1 lettuce

1⅓ pint/800 ml stock
Seasoning
1 tablespoon *tofu* or yoghurt

Peel and finely chop the onion. Sweat it in a pan until translucent. Add the sliced courgettes and continue to cook on a very low heat for a few minutes. Pick over and wash the lettuce and remove any damaged outer leaves. Tear the rest into pieces and add to the pan. Moisten with a little stock and cook gently for a further 2 minutes, by which time the lettuce should be soft, but still green. Cool a little and put into the blender with half the stock and the *tofu* or yoghurt. Blend until smooth. I think it is not necessary to sieve this kind of soup. Stir in the rest of the stock, season to taste and then finish off according to whether you are serving the soup cold or hot.

HOT SOUPS

Tomato and beetroot soup
SERVES 4–6

This soup is similar to borscht in flavour since it uses beetroot as its main ingredient, but the addition of a thick tomato *coulis* just before serving enriches both texture and colour. Any left-over soup can be made into a purée in the blender and served as a delicious sauce for poached or grilled white fish.

1 onion	1 tablespoon oil – optional
1 carrot	Pinch of dill seed or dill weed
1 stick celery	1 pint / 600 ml stock
1 leek	1 lb / 450 g tomatoes
1 small turnip	Seasoning
¾ lb / 350 g beetroot	

Peel, then slice or dice the vegetables quite small. Sweat them in the oil in a heavy saucepan (or use a non-stick pan) for 5 minutes. Stir in the herbs and the stock. Cook for 30–40 minutes, until the vegetables are tender. In another saucepan cook the roughly chopped tomatoes for 5 minutes or so, until the juices run. Put in the blender and make into a purée. Rub this through a sieve into the pot of beetroot soup. Bring to the boil, stir thoroughly and serve at once.

Potato, basil and pea soup
SERVES 4

A warming, nourishing soup for a cool summer's day.

1 lb / 450 g potatoes	Seasoning
1⅓ pint / 800 ml vegetable or chicken stock	1 tablespoon skimmed milk powder
4 oz / 100 g fresh shelled peas	12 large basil leaves

Peel or scrub the potatoes, dice them and cook them until soft in the stock. Put a little stock and at least half the cooked potato in a blender or food processor and process until smooth. Return this purée to the rest of the soup, reserving about 2 tablespoons of stock. Bring the soup to the boil and add the peas. Simmer these for 2 or 3 minutes. Season to taste. Meanwhile blend the skimmed milk powder with the reserved stock and stir this into the soup. Tear up the basil leaves into shreds and stir these into the boiling soup. Serve immediately.

A very simple soup, with a delicate flavour of fennel and barely a hint of apple. Cook in a non-stick saucepan.

Carrot, fennel and apple soup
SERVES 4

½ lb/225 g carrots
6 oz/175 g fennel
1 dessert apple

1⅓ pints/800 ml stock
Seasoning

Peel and slice the carrots. Trim and slice the fennel. Quarter, core and slice the apple. Sweat the vegetables and apple in a little stock until soft. Put in the blender or food processor and process until smooth. Reheat and season to taste. Serve immediately.

This light and most nourishing of soups exists in similar forms throughout southern Europe. In Portugal the *sopa alentejana* has a raw egg slid into a bowl of piping hot broth flavoured with garlic and coriander. Italy's soup from Pavia, *zuppa Pavese*, has an egg on a large *croûton* in a richer, chickeny broth. Garlic is the main ingredient in Spain's *sopa de ajo*, the broth being flavoured with a little ham, the egg cooking in the boiling liquid and often served in an earthenware bowl. In Malta the soup is named *soppa tal-armla*, widow's soup, and was a dish traditionally offered to the poor of the parish. The soup bowl would contain, as well as a poached egg in vegetable broth, a small sheep's cheese and the shredded cooked vegetables.

Egg soup

It is a good supper or lunch dish when you don't feel like making anything complicated. Per person you need an earthenware bowl and

⅓ pint/200 ml stock
1 clove garlic
Fresh herbs

Flavouring or garnish
1 egg

Lightly oil the soup bowl and heat it. Heat the stock to boiling point. Crush the garlic and add it to the stock with some fresh herbs. Add the flavouring or garnish which could be a handful of tiny new peas, a tablespoon of skinned chopped tomato, some diced ham or sausage, or what you will. Crack the egg into the heated soup bowl and carefully pour on the boiling stock and flavouring. Allow to stand for a minute to let the egg continue cooking. Serve with crusty bread.

Salmon and
dill consommé
SERVES 4

Reflecting on ways of making light, yet substantial and, above all, interesting soups, I was thinking about how one bakes a *soupe à l'oignon* in the oven to get that lovely golden topping. Were there other ways of 'topping' a soup? Pie crusts yes, but even lighter would be a soufflé, and so I top this clear consommé with a salmon soufflé. It is a good dish to make after you have poached a whole salmon and have some left over. Save the poaching liquid, boil up the salmon head and bones in it to give you the stock for this recipe, which you will then need to clarify, either with egg whites or through a dampened coffee filter paper.

1⅓ pints/800 ml good salmon
   stock plus 2 extra
   tablespoons
1 bunch dill weed
8 oz/225 g cooked salmon

1 tablespoon double cream
Seasoning
1 teaspoon cornflour
4 size-3 eggs

Heat the stock and infuse in it half the dill while you prepare the soufflé. Put the cooked salmon in the food processor with the cream and a tablespoon of stock. Sieve into a basin and season to taste. Blend the cornflour with a tablespoon of stock and add it to the salmon mixture. Separate the eggs. Beat the yolks into the salmon mixture and whisk the egg whites until stiff and fold into the fish.

Remove the dill from the salmon stock and divide the stock among four ovenproof soup bowls. Snip the rest of the dill into the bowls and spoon the soufflé mixture on top of each bowl, smoothing it to the rim of the bowl. Bake in a pre-heated oven, 200°C/400°F/gas mark 6, for 10–12 minutes.

Scallop and
vanilla soup
with coral
SERVES 6

This rich, yet delicately flavoured soup makes a wonderful starter for a dinner party with its swirl of coral cream on the surface, and elusive vanilla flavour.

8 plump scallops with plenty
   of roe
3 shallots
2 pints/1.2 litres fish stock

1 vanilla pod
Seasoning
⅓ teaspoon cornflour
1 tablespoon Greek yoghurt

Trim and wash the scallops, removing the small pad of muscle. Peel and chop the shallots. Take 1 pint/600 ml stock and poach the scallops, the roe and the shallots and the split vanilla pod. Remove the scallops and roe after 2 minutes and simmer the shallots and vanilla for a little longer, say 10 minutes. Remove the vanilla pod, wash it and dry it for use another time.

Dice 2 of the scallops and set these aside with the roe. Put the rest of the scallops, the shallots and most of the stock in the blender and process until smooth. Season to taste. Blend the rest of the stock with the scallop roe to make a smooth orange cream. Mix the cornflour with the yoghurt and stir it into the scallop soup. Heat gently, and gradually bring to the boil. Gently heat the coral cream in a saucepan without bringing it to the boil. Pour the soup into heated soup plates and pour a swirl of coral sauce into each. Serve immediately.

Fish stock and left-over fish combine with fresh fennel to make a delicate, creamy soup. It is delicious cold, but I like to serve it hot on one of those typically chilly, English summer days.

Salmon trout and fennel soup
SERVES 4

1 fennel bulb	Seasoning
1⅓ pints/800 ml fish stock	4 oz/100 g cooked salmon
1 tablespoon *fromage frais* or	trout
thick plain yoghurt	

Try to find a fennel bulb with plenty of green tops. Cut these off and reserve them for garnish. Trim the bulb, removing any discoloured, stringy bits. Dice it and place in a saucepan. Pour on a quarter of the stock and cook gently until the fennel is soft. Put it into a blender with the *fromage frais* or yoghurt and the rest of the stock. If you wish you can add the fish at this stage to give a thick, creamy, smooth soup, or you can flake the fish into the soup as you reheat it. Blend the soup and sieve it back into the saucepan. Reheat gently, season to taste and serve immediately, garnished with the finely chopped fennel tops.

A tiny drop of Pernod or *anis* flavoured liquor can be added as you are reheating the soup to intensify the fennel flavour.

*Game broth
with dumplings*
SERVES 4

This is a good way of making use of leftovers such as carcasses, bones and trimmings from a venison roast, or legs from pigeons or partridges from a dish which requires the breasts only.

1½ lb/675 g bones and
   trimmings of game
1 carrot
1 leek
1 onion
1 stick celery
2 pints/1.2 litres water
¼ pint/150 ml wine
Bundle of mixed herbs

For the dumplings:
3 oz/75 g wholemeal flour
½ teaspoon baking powder
1½ oz/40 g *fromage blanc* or
   sieved cottage cheese
1 oz/25 g minced cooked
   game
Good pinch thyme
Seasoning, including nutmeg

Brown the bones and vegetables. Pour on the water and wine and add the herbs. Simmer gently for at least 2 hours, skimming the surface from time to time to remove any impurities. Strain the stock and then pour it through a sieve lined with damp cheesecloth. If you want a clearer broth, you can then clarify it using whisked egg white. Reduce the broth to 1⅓ pints/800 ml.

To make the dumplings, mix all the ingredients together and form into balls the size of hazelnuts. Bring a pan of water to the boil then turn it down to a gentle simmer. Put the dumplings in carefully and simmer gently. When cooked they will float to the top. Divide amongst heated soup plates and pour the broth over them, checking for seasoning first.

*Festive
borscht and
piroshkis*
SERVES 6–8

A recipe for using up left-over turkey and its stock. Other kinds of meat and stock can be used of course.

1 tablespoon olive oil
1 large onion
1 carrot
1 stick celery
1 leek
¾ lb/350 g beetroot, peeled
   and diced
¾ lb/350 g tomatoes or 1 tin
   peeled plum tomatoes,
   roughly chopped

3 cloves garlic
½ tsp dill seeds or dill weed
3 pints/1.8 litres stock
6 oz/175 g cooked meat
6 oz/175 g puff, flaky or
   shortcrust pastry
sour cream or smatana

Melt the fat in a large saucepan and stir in the first four vegetables, all thinly sliced. Cook until lightly browning. Add the beetroot, tomatoes, crushed garlic and dill. Pour in the stock, bring to the boil and simmer gently for 40 minutes, or until the vegetables are soft.

Scoop out a few of the vegetables and process with the cooked meat to moisten and flavour it. Season if necessary.

Roll out the pastry and cut into rounds or squares. Place à teaspoon of the meat mixture in the centre. Moisten the edges of the pastry, fold over and seal. Brush with milk or melted butter, place on a baking sheet and bake in a hot oven for 10–12 minutes.

Hand piping hot with the soup, which you can either serve as it is, vegetables and all, or you can strain it and serve a clear soup. Either way, a spoonful of sour cream or smatana is quite a nice addition. Strained and allowed to go cold, you can then remove any fat, add an ice cube or two and serve chilled borscht.

My favourite drink with this is tiny, chilled glasses of the best vodka.

Hare, like other game, has a particular affinity with root vegetables. Parsnips, turnips, potatoes, Jerusalem artichokes can all be used to thicken the soup. Here I use celeriac.

Hare soup
SERVES 4

1 rasher smoked bacon	1⅓ pint/800 ml game stock
1 onion	made from the carcass of the
¾ lb/350 g celeriac	hare
	Seasoning

Cut the bacon into 1 in/2.5 cm strips. Heat them in a heavy saucepan until the fat begins to run. Peel and slice the onion and add to the pan. Allow to brown slightly but not burn. Peel the celeriac and cut it into smallish dice. Add this to the onion and turn it in the bacon fat. Pour on the stock, together with any left-over gravy, sauce, marinade, pieces of meat and cook until the celeriac is tender. Put through a *mouli légumes* or blender and season to taste.

Black bean
and bacon soup
SERVES 6

This is an ideal soup to cook in a clay pot; long slow cooking will tenderise the beans and extract maximum flavour from the bacon. Use smoked or green bacon according to your preference.

¾ lb / 350 g black beans
1 knuckle of bacon
1 tablespoon olive oil
2–3 cloves garlic
1 onion
½ teaspoon powdered ginger or
   crushed fresh ginger
1 tablespoon clear honey
Freshly ground black pepper
2½ pints / 1.5 litres water

Soak the beans overnight. Next day soak the bacon for an hour to remove excess saltiness. Throw the water away. Drain the beans and add to the bacon in the bottom half of a clay pot. Make sure you have soaked it first in cold water for 10–15 minutes. Heat the olive oil in a small frying pan. Peel and slice the garlic and onion and fry until lightly golden. Stir in the ginger, honey and black pepper and moisten with ¼ pint / 150 ml water and make into a sauce. Pour this over the beans. Bring the rest of the water to the boil and pour it over the beans. Cover with the lid and cook in the bottom of a slow oven, 170°C / 325°F / gas mark 3, for 4–5 hours. Leaving it all day will not harm it and will make the kitchen smell wonderful on your return. Add more water or stock if necessary. Serve straight from the pot. Salad before, bread with, and fruit after makes this into a cheap, nourishing meal.

Vegetables

Readers will find many omissions from this section. Where are all the recipes for asparagus, avocado pears, broccoli, cauliflower, courgettes, and mangetouts? Apart from a couple of salad recipes, I have not dealt with them because I feel that the best way of cooking these and most vegetables is to quickly prepare them, quickly cook them in lightly salted fast-boiling water and serve them immediately. Food processors make our task easier. Mine slices carrots and celery far more quickly than I can, and I truly believe that with vegetables you must work quickly once you've peeled them or otherwise got started on their preparation. A new electric steamer is now available in Britain and this cooks vegetables beautifully (as it does fish and other ingredients of course). Large enough to take even the longest asparagus stalks lying flat, this is going to become a much used piece of kitchen equipment, elevated beyond some of the gadgetry which I have relegated to the far recesses of my bottom cupboards. Not that an electric steamer is essential; a traditional one does an excellent job too.

What I have tried to do in this chapter is give some ideas of how to use vegetables as starters and main courses, as well as an accompaniment playing second fiddle to the main meat or fish dish. I have also tended to concentrate on some of our more common vegetables, those which are cheap and widely available, but I have used them in less traditional ways.

Too often, unless we are vegetarians, we think of vegetables as an afterthought and rarely exploit their full potential. This is one more reason why I like the Italian way of eating. There vegetables figure much more prominently in the menu as dishes in their own right. Think about what they can add to a meal. No other ingredient comes in so many shapes, colours and textures.

LEAFY PARCELS

Little green packets with hidden stuffings are fun to make if you have plenty of time at your disposal, and they are much appreciated as snacks with drinks, starters or a vegetable course.

Almost any green, leafy vegetable can be used as the wrapping; spinach, chard, lettuce, cabbage and even leeks if they are the big, fat variety. Whatever you use, make sure it is fresh, firm and whole. Remove the central stem if your chosen vegetable has one, as this prevents you from making a neat parcel. I think it is a good idea to blanch the greens first as it makes them more pliable and less likely to split. The easiest way to do this is to drape the leaves over a colander or sieve and gently pour boiling water over them. Drain and lay on a tea-towel to dry, patting them gently with kitchen paper.

The amount of stuffing will depend on the size of the leaf and whether or not the parcel is to be a bite-sized appetiser or a more substantial first course. A teaspoonful of stuffing is sufficient for the former, a dessertspoonful for the latter. Spoon the stuffing on to the leaf, veined side up and roll into a neat cork-shaped parcel. Place in a lightly oiled baking dish, with the opening underneath. Continue until you have used up all the leaves and stuffing. Then cover with greaseproof paper, perhaps sprinkling with a little olive oil, wine or stock as appropriate and bake in a medium hot oven 190°C/375°F/ gas mark 5. Serve hot or cold.

Here are some combinations that I think work particularly well:

Spinach – stuffed with cooked brown rice, olives and fresh mint, served with a tomato *coulis* (see p. 54).

Chard – stuffed with ricotta, blue cheese and chopped walnuts and brown breadcrumbs, served hot as appetisers.

Lettuce – stuffed with beansprouts, freshly grated ginger and prawns, served with a dip of soy sauce and rice vinegar.

Leeks – stuffed with cooked, flaked, smoked haddock mixed with mashed potatoes and garlic.

Here is a rather grand recipe for cabbage stuffed with a mushroom mousseline, which is wonderful with game birds such as partridge or pheasant. If you can get fresh wild mushrooms so much the better. If not, the flavour of dried wild mushrooms is an important addition, and worth the extra money; dried wild mushrooms are really quite economical, go a long way, keep well and just one small piece of dried *porcini* snipped into a soup or casserole immediately enhances the flavour.

Cabbage parcels stuffed with mushroom mousseline
MAKES 8

½ oz/10–15 g dried wild mushrooms	2 shallots
½ pint/300 ml stock	1 egg
8 large cabbage leaves	Seasoning
8 oz/225 g fresh mushrooms	6 juniper berries
4 oz/100 g ricotta	1 sprig rosemary

Cut the dried mushrooms into small pieces, place them in a basin and pour on the boiling stock. Cut the hard central rib from each cabbage leaf and blanch the leaves thoroughly. Wipe the fresh mushrooms, only peeling if absolutely necessary, and chop them very fine. (I use a food processor at this point.) Mix thoroughly with the ricotta. Peel and finely chop the shallots and add these to the mushroom and cheese mixture. Separate the egg. Beat the yolk lightly and stir this into the mixture. Season to taste. Whisk the egg white and fold this in. Strain the dried wild mushroom pieces, reserving the liquor, and stir them in gently.

Divide the stuffing among the eight cabbage leaves and roll into neat parcels. Place in a lightly oiled baking dish. Scatter the juniper berries and lay the sprig of rosemary on the cabbage parcels and sprinkle with mushroom liquor. Cover with foil and bake in a pre-heated oven, 190°C/375°F/gas mark 5, for 25 minutes. Serve hot.

Aubergine
salad
SERVES 4

This is a quick, easy, inexpensive starter; a purée of aubergine, herbs and garlic. Hot, it would make a most appropriate accompaniment to grilled lamb, either kebabs or *noisettes*. And it is delicious stirred into freshly cooked pasta.

1 lb/450 g aubergine
Cloves of garlic to taste
3 heaped tablespoons finely chopped parsley

Pinch of fresh or dried thyme or oregano
Seasoning

Slice the aubergine in half down its length. Get the grill very hot and put the aubergine under it, skin side to the flame. Grill for 15 minutes until the skin is wrinkled and charred (but not burnt). This is, of course, difficult to see, but your sense of touch and smell will tell you when it is charred. Remove from the grill and when cool enough to handle, scoop out the softened flesh with a pointed teaspoon. Put this in a sieve over a basin so that some of the liquid drains away. The flesh tends to come away in long strands, so snip these up with kitchen scissors. Peel and crush the garlic cloves and stir into the aubergine. Add the herbs and season to taste.

Serve as it is, with hot toast or warm pitta bread, or on a plate of salad leaves garnished with olives and tomatoes.

Salad of
quail eggs in
tarragon jelly
SERVES 4 or 6

A summer dish to make if you have lots of tarragon available. Use only French tarragon. The almost rank flavour of Russian tarragon is not appropriate. I do not understand why it is grown and sold.

½ pint/300 ml good clear stock
Bunch of tarragon
12 quail eggs

4 sheets gelatine
Salad leaves

Bring half the stock to the boil. Remove a dozen or so of the best tarragon leaves. Roughly chop the rest and add to the stock. Boil for 2 minutes, remove from the heat and let infuse for 15–20 minutes. Bring a pan of water to the boil, gently slide in the quail eggs. Boil them for 30 seconds. Remove from the heat and leave for 2 minutes before plunging the eggs into cold water. Soften the gelatine in the rest of the stock, and then gently melt over heat.

Strain the tarragon stock into the gelatine stock and mix thoroughly. Pour a little into four or six small ramekins. Allow to set. Lay tarragon leaves on top. Shell the quail eggs and put two or three in each ramekin. Fill to the top with the rest of the cooled stock. Allow to set. To serve, arrange a bed of salad leaves on each individual plate. Unmould the jellies by briefly dipping the base of the ramekins in hot water, and turn out on to the salad leaves.

Wild mushrooms in blackberry vinegar
SERVES 4–6

This is a dish full of wild, woodland flavours. First make your blackberry vinegar. Take a pound of fresh, ripe, wild blackberries, which although they are often tough and woody, have an intenser flavour than the cultivated kind. Tip them into a deep pudding basin, after you have removed any signs of wild life. Roughly crush them with the back of a wooden spoon. Pour on a bottle of good quality wine vinegar, red or white. Cover with muslin or a folded tea-towel and leave for a couple of days. Strain through muslin and put into bottles.

If you cannot get wild mushrooms, cultivated ones will do. Some supermarkets and greengrocers now stock oyster mushrooms (*pleurottes*) grown in Holland.

1 lb/450 g mushrooms
1 mild, sweet onion
Salt
Pepper

5 tablespoons walnut oil
3 tablespoons blackberry
vinegar

Slice the mushrooms and onion. Mix together gently so you don't break them up and pile in a white china dish. Sprinkle with salt and pepper. Heat the oil and vinegar to almost boiling point. Pour over the mushrooms and leave it all to go cold. Serve as a salad with brown bread and butter. Finely chopped parsley or a *chiffonade* of fresh basil to garnish.

This method can be used for other marinated vegetable salads. The following are good combinations: thin slices or batons of carrots in honey and cider vinegar and hazelnut oil; *haricots verts* in balsamic vinegar and sunflower oil with toasted sunflower seeds; charred peeled green peppers in sherry vinegar and olive oil.

Mixed Green capsicums, grilled to remove the skins and then served in olive
pepper salad oil is one of my favourite dishes of *tapas* in Spain, the wide array of
SERVES 4 snacks and appetisers from which you choose something to eat
while you drink deliciously dry, crisp sherry before lunch. I am
reminded particularly of a tiny restaurant in Jerez de la Frontera
where the *tapas* would have made a meal in themselves and where
the sherry was, as we had been led to expect, of a flavour, freshness
and delicacy that is hard to find here.

From Holland we now import capsicums not only green, but also
yellow, red and black. A striking salad can be made with these, to
serve as a first course rather than as an accompanying dish.

4 capsicums, about 5 oz/150 g each	1 teaspoon sherry vinegar or wine vinegar
1 clove garlic, optional	Seasoning
2 tablespoons olive oil	

Cut the capsicums in half and remove the stalk and seeds. Arrange
them on a grill rack, flattening them slightly. Put under a hot grill
until the skins are charred and blackened all over. This takes about
5 minutes. Remove from the heat and put all the peppers in a paper
bag. Close it and allow the steam to build up to help loosen the skin.

Now for the tedious part which is to remove every scrap of skin
from the peppers. The heat from the grill will have cooked them
slightly and the charring gives them a delicious flavour. Cut the
capsicums into strips, say 1 in/2.5 cm wide, and arrange on a
platter. Crush the garlic and mix it with the oil, vinegar and
seasoning. Sprinkle it over the peppers and let them stand in a cool
place, not the refrigerator, for at least 30 minutes to bring out and
develop the flavours.

Spinach and
walnut salad
SERVES 4

1 lb/450 g spinach	4 tablespoons walnut oil
4 oz/100 g walnuts	Lemon juice or fruit vinegar
2 cloves garlic	Seasoning

Pick over the spinach. Discard any tough, broken or discoloured
leaves. Discard the stalks from the longer leaves and tear them into
two or three pieces. Keep the small, tender leaves whole. Wash and

dry thoroughly, preferably in a salad spinner. Place in a salad bowl.

Chop the walnuts. Crush the garlic and stir with the walnuts into the walnut oil. Blend in the lemon juice or vinegar and season to taste. Pour over the spinach. Toss and serve immediately.

Vegetable terrine
SERVES 8–12

4–5 oz/125 g uncooked chicken breast
1 egg white
Seasoning
1 tablespoon sunflower oil
Juice of half a lemon
1 tablespoon chervil or flat leaf parsley
8 oz/225 g tender, trimmed leeks

7 oz/200 g button or oyster mushrooms
7 oz/200 g fennel
4 oz/100 g red pepper
4 oz/100 g spinach
5–6 oz/150 g tomatoes
1 pint/600 ml vegetable or chicken stock

First, prepare and cook each vegetable, except for the tomatoes, in the stock, separately, until tender, drain and allow to cool. Strip the outer leaves from the leeks; wipe the mushrooms; trim the fennel; cut the pepper in quarters, lengthways and remove the stalk and seeds; wash and drain the spinach before cooking it. Peel, de-seed, chop the tomatoes and allow them to drain. For the next stage use a food processor. Cut the skinned and boned chicken breasts into chunks and process until smooth. Add the egg white, seasoning and lemon juice and process again. Add the oil a little at a time as if making mayonnaise.

Line a 2 lb/1 kg terrine or loaf tin, base and sides, with part of the chicken mixture. Place the vegetables in successive layers in the terrine, keeping each vegetable separate. In order to give the terrine a good shape when cooked, prepare the vegetables as follows; slice the leeks lengthwise, quarter the mushrooms, slice the fennel into $\frac{1}{4}$ in/5 mm thick slices, press and chop the spinach.

Cover the last layer of vegetables with the remaining chicken mixture. Place in a roasting tin containing 1–2 in/2.5–5 cm water and bake in a pre-heated oven, 150–170°C/300–325°F/gas mark 2–3, for $1\frac{1}{4}$ hours. Remove from the oven, cool completely, cover and keep in the refrigerator until required. Garnish with parsley or chervil

Asparagus and mangetout salad with prawns and warm sesame dressing
SERVES 6

2 oz/50 g salad leaves is enough for one serving. Use a mixture of whatever you can find. Oak leaf, Salad Bowl, Little Gem are all good lettuces; if you can, add some *mâche* (corn salad), radicchio, watercress etc. This is not intended to cover the plate but, rather, to provide a bed of green and red for the prawns to rest on. For the dressing I like to use a fruit vinegar such as blackcurrant, raspberry or blackberry. You could use cider vinegar, lime or lemon juice or rice vinegar instead.

1 lb/450 g not too thick asparagus
½ lb/225 g mangetouts
1 teaspoon sesame oil
2 dessertspoons olive oil
2–3 cloves garlic

12 oz/350 g washed and dried salad leaves
1 lb/450 g Greenland prawns, defrosted
1 dessertspoon vinegar

Snap off the tenderest part of the asparagus, say about 4–5 in/10–12 cms. It will not need peeling. Top and tail the mangetouts and pull off the stringy edges if necessary. Place a steamer over a pan of boiling water and lay the asparagus on it. Cover and steam for 5–8 minutes, then add the mangetouts and steam for a further 4 minutes. Meanwhile peel and crush the garlic. Heat the oils in a frying pan and, when hot, add the garlic. Remove immediately from the heat.

Remove the vegetables from the steamer and arrange decoratively on individual plates (dinner plates, not side plates, or everything will look too crowded). Arrange a small bed of salad leaves on the plate. Heat up the oil again and when almost smoking add the prawns. Stir-fry for 2–3 minutes only. The prawns have already been cooked, remember. Add the flavoured vinegar to the pan, shake, remove from the heat and divide the prawns between the plates, on the salad leaves. Pour the hot dressing over the salad and serve immediately.

Vegetable platter
SERVES 4

This is simply a plate of *crudités*, as carefully and elegantly prepared as possible, served on a bed of cracked ice with a delicious and unusual dip made from *tofu*, soya bean curd, which has a creamy texture and little flavour of its own but makes the perfect base for a herb cream. It is sold in delicatessens, health food shops and shops which sell food from China and Japan. Use whatever fresh herbs are available – chervil, coriander, parsley, chives, tarragon.

4 oz/125 g *tofu*	Garlic to taste
4 shallots	Good handful of green herbs
Pinch of fresh or powdered ginger	Salt, pepper, paprika

Put all the ingredients in the blender or food processor and process until smooth. Serve with the vegetables.

This also makes an excellent sauce to accompany cold fish dishes.

For this dish, choose a variety of crunchy vegetables which you can quickly prepare. I like to use the following; the amounts I give here are approximate.

Sesame salad
SERVES 5–6

4 oz/125 g Jerusalem artichokes	2 cloves garlic – optional
4 oz/125 g white radish	2 tablespoons sesame oil
4 oz/125 g carrots	4 tablespoons apple juice
4 oz/125 g beansprouts	2 tablespoons toasted sesame seeds
4 oz/125 g sweet peppers	

Working quickly, trim, wash, slice or shred the vegetables as appropriate. I find the Jerusalem artichokes are best peeled and sliced wafer thin, or shredded. Sprinkle them with some of the apple juice to keep them pale. Arrange the vegetables either on individual plates or on one platter, perhaps in wedges of colour. Mix the garlic, oil, apple juice and sesame seeds, pour over the vegetables and serve immediately.

Sunflower seeds (and oil) can be substituted for the sesame seeds and oil.

These three combine usually to make an Italian salad. I rarely serve avocados, and even more rarely do I cook them, believing that a buttery, ripe avocado is best with a little black pepper and lemon juice. But one day, having prepared my salad *tricolore*, in neat overlapping slices, I changed my mind and wanted a hot dish, so stuck the (fortunately for me) earthenware platter in a hot oven and produced a rather tasty, melting concoction.

Hot avocado, tomato and mozzarella
SERVES 4–6

2 ripe avocados	2 mozzarella cheeses
½ lemon	Seasoning
4 firm tomatoes	

Cut the avocados in half, remove the stones, peel and slice. Sprinkle the slices with lemon juice. Peel and slice the tomatoes. Slice the mozzarella. Place a layer of avocado slices in an earthenware or other ovenproof dish, arrange a layer of tomatoes on top and season lightly with salt and pepper. Lay the mozzarella slices on top and place the dish in a hot oven, 200°C/400°F/gas mark 6, for 15–20 minutes, until bubbling and golden brown.

Baked field mushrooms
SERVES 4

These velvety, soft, dark mushrooms have a good deal more flavour than the cup and button mushrooms. But how to keep the scent from disappearing into the oven? Sealing it in a paper bag is the answer.

They make an inexpensive and easy starter; they can be prepared well in advance and set aside in a cool place until required. What you stuff them with is a matter of choice. Snail butter is, of course, delicious. Cooked rice or brown breadcrumbs will make a more substantial dish and soak up some of the juice. Left-over wild rice would be just about perfect.

4 tablespoons olive oil or melted butter	4 tablespoons cooked rice
4 large field mushrooms	2 tablespoons finely chopped parsley
4 cloves garlic	Seasoning
2 shallots	

Cut four 15 x 20 in/40 x 50 cm rectangles from baking parchment and fold each in half down the middle. Cut each piece of paper into a heart shape with the fold running down to the point. Brush some of the olive oil or butter on the papers and put the rest in a basin. Wipe and, if necessary, peel the mushrooms. Remove the stalk and chop this finely. Peel and finely chop the garlic and the shallots and mix them with the stalk, the cooked rice, the rest of the olive oil or butter, parsley and seasoning. Divide amongst the four mushroom caps, packing the mixture well down. Put one mushroom cap on each paper heart. The parcels are now ready to seal. Fold over the other side of the heart. With the edges together fold the paper over, making tight overlapping folds, or rolling the edges together to seal the parcel. Prepare the other parcels in the same way and lay them on a baking tray. Place it in a pre-heated oven, 200°C/400°F/gas mark 6, for 10 minutes. Serve while hot, placing each parcel on an individual plate and cutting it open at the table.

Timbale of parsnip with fruit jelly
SERVES 4–6

Enhance the sweetness of a parsnip purée by burying a spoonful of fruit jelly in the centre and serve it as an inexpensive but unusual side dish with game or poultry.

1lb/450 g parsnips
1 size-3 egg, separated

4–6 teaspoons home-made fruit jelly

Peel, slice and boil the parsnips until soft. Mash them thoroughly and beat in the egg yolk. Whisk the egg white and fold gently into the parsnip. Divide the mixture amongst four or six lightly oiled dariole moulds, or ramekins. Make a well in the purée and spoon in a little jelly, covering with more parsnip. Place in a *bain-marie* and cook for 15 minutes. Turn out on to heated plates.

Steamed cucumber
SERVES 4–6

This makes a very light, simple and unusual vegetable dish, perfect as a garnish for fish and chicken dishes.

1 cucumber
Seasoning
1 teaspoon dill seeds

Peel the cucumber and cut it into three or four 4 in/10 cm chunks. Cut each in half, vertically, and remove the seeds. Slice each piece into sticks or batons. Season lightly and place in a steamer basket. Add the cucumber peel to the water in the steamer, and sprinkle dill seeds on the cucumber. Steam it for 5 or 6 minutes and serve immediately.

Timbales of sweet potatoes with ceps
SERVES 4

These elongated tubers with dusky red skin are more and more available in shops which provide for West African, Caribbean and Asian communities. Sweet, orange fleshed, they make an unusual accompaniment to game and poultry. In America they are tradition-ally served glazed or candied with the Thanksgiving turkey, but this is something I can never get used to. I much prefer my mother-in-law's delicious mashed potato. Candying the potatoes makes them just too sweet for me and I would rather see them at the pudding stage prepared pumpkin-style in a spicy pie.

Here I prepare them with a tiny quantity of fragrant wild mushrooms. Dried ceps work almost better than fresh, in that their aroma is more concentrated.

Scant ½ oz/10 g dried ceps   1 size-3 egg
1 lb/450 g sweet potatoes   Seasoning

Snip the mushrooms into tiny pieces and put to soak in boiling water. Wash the potatoes thoroughly and boil in their skins. Cooking time will depend on their size. When done, drain and allow to cool slightly. Cut in half and scoop all the flesh into a basin. Mash. Drain the ceps and add these to the mashed sweet potato. Separate the egg. Beat the yolk into the potato. Whisk the egg white and fold this gently into the mixture. Fill four lightly oiled timbales with the mixture. Level it off and place in a *bain-marie* in a moderate oven, 180°C/350°F/gas mark 4, for 15 minutes. To serve, turn out on to individual dinner plates to accompany your chosen main course.

Orange glazed turnips
SERVES 4

I have only ever made this dish with small white turnips and am not sure if the large, yellow ones would be as delicious. White radish or mooli would lend itself to the same method of preparation. It accompanies game and poultry very well.

1 lb/450 g small white turnips
2 oranges
Black pepper

Thinly peel and slice the turnips. Grate some of the zest from the oranges, cut in half and squeeze the juice into a saucepan. Bring to the boil, drop in the turnip slices and cook, covered, over a low heat until tender but not squashy, and the sauce is syrupy. Serve sprinkled with a little orange zest and some ground black pepper.

A variation on this above recipe is to use a sweeter vegetable and a sharper fruit. Prepare sweet potatoes as above and use the juice and zest of 1 lime, adding equal quantities of water. Prepare lemon glazed beetroot and grapefruit glazed carrots or parsnips in the same way.

Don't waste new potatoes and carrots on a purée. The older, larger ones will do.

Carrot and potato purée
SERVES 4

½ lb/225 g carrots   3 heads of garlic
½ lb/225 g potatoes   6 cardamom pods

Peel all the vegetables. Cut the potatoes and carrots into chunks and boil them together with the peeled garlic and the seeds from the cardamom pods. When soft, drain and mash.

Not really a jam, although I daresay one could make a very good potted preserve from shallots and beetroot, this is a nicely sweet and sour accompaniment for poultry or game dishes. For the 'sour' I use a home-made blackcurrant vinegar; any fruit or herb vinegar will do, but of course a fruit vinegar will generally add a little more sweetness.

Beetroot and shallot 'jam'
SERVES 6–8

4 oz/100 g beetroot   2 tablespoons fruit vinegar
4 oz/100 g shallots   Freshly ground black pepper

Using a small non-stick saucepan will avoid the need for butter or oil. Peel and chop the vegetables into very small dice. There should be nothing 'chunky' about this at all. If you can't make tiny enough dice, then use a coarse grater. Sweat the vegetables until soft, say 10–15 minutes. Add the vinegar and turn up the heat to reduce the liquid to a shiny glaze which coats the beetroot and shallot mixture. Season with black pepper. Serve hot.

This might, I think, make an excellent (cold) relish for cold meats, such as spiced beef or roast ham or turkey.

This dish was first cooked for me by John and June Day in Dulverton. Its outward appearance is as important as the flavour of the finished product, so choose vegetables with the best skins, i.e. good colour, form, no blemishes, fresh and shiny. Suitable for stuffing are onions, aubergines, sweet peppers (capsicums) in all their many colours, squashes, and even cabbages. How many to serve per person? This depends very much on the size. For preference choose smaller vegetables so that you could serve two or three kinds to each guest, perhaps an onion, a pepper and a small aubergine.

Stuffed vegetables

Prepare the stuffing first to let the flavours mingle and develop. Here is a recipe for vegetarians, and one for meat-eaters.

If you are preparing the stuffing in very large quantities, mix a little first and taste it to see that you have the proportions and seasoning as you want them. It would be such a waste to prepare several pounds of stuffing and find it wasn't quite right.

Vegetarian stuffing
Use aubergine only if you are stuffing aubergines; if not, increase the quantity of tomato, or add chopped red or green pepper or more onion.

For *each* medium sized vegetable:

2 oz/50 g cooked brown rice
1 oz/25 g peeled, seeded, chopped tomato
1 oz/25 g finely chopped onion
½ oz/15 g stoned, roughly chopped olives

½ oz/15 g chopped aubergine
Garlic, salt and pepper to taste
Fresh herbs, a teaspoon of whatever you have available
Olive oil, just sufficient to moisten the mixture

Mix all the ingredients together and allow to stand, covered, in a cool place while you prepare the vegetables.

Meat stuffing
If you are preparing this recipe when fresh mint is not available there are a couple of ways of enlivening dried mint. One tip is to bruise it over coarse salt. I find that crushing a large quantity of dried mint with a few grains of sugar and then infusing it in a few tablespoons of boiling water also brings the flavour out. The meat used can be whatever you prefer – beef, veal, pork, lamb or a mixture.

2 oz/50 g lean, raw, minced meat
1 oz/25 g cooked brown rice

1 oz/25 g chopped onion
1 oz/25 g chopped fresh mint
Salt and pepper to taste

Mix all the ingredients thoroughly and put to one side while you prepare the vegetables. Olive oil is not necessary here because the meat, even the leanest, will give off some fat in cooking.

Preparation of vegetables for stuffing
Peppers – Choose regular shaped ones that will stand upright if

possible. Cut a shallow cap from the stalk end. Remove the white pith and seeds from the hollow pepper and its cap. It is now ready to stuff.

Onions – Peel the onion and remove a thin slice from top and bottom. Score down vertically through two layers of skin only, and carefully remove the two outer layers. Tie kitchen thread round the middle and you are left with a hollowed out onion to fill. The centre part of the onion which you have removed can be finely chopped and added to the stuffing.

Aubergines – To prepare these you need a small sharp knife and a small pointed teaspoon. Even better would be implements with serrated edges of the kind used to prepare and eat grapefruits. Cut a thin slice from the bottom of the aubergine to allow it to stand upright. Cut a slice off the top to make a cap – about $\frac{3}{4}$ in/ $1\frac{1}{2}$ cm or so. Then, with your sharp pointed implements, hollow out the aubergine leaving a thin shell about $\frac{1}{4}$ in/ $\frac{1}{2}$ cm thick. Chop what you scoop out and add this to the stuffing. Lightly salt and pepper the hollowed out shell and turn upside down for any juices to drain off.

Cabbage – If the cabbage is large it will have large outer leaves. In this case remove as many single leaves as you wish, wash them and cut out the base of the central stem if it is very tough. The leaves are now ready for stuffing individually.

If the cabbage is a small, tight one, cut off a slice from the stalk end. With your sharpest small knife, hollow out the cabbage, leaving the outer leaves as the casing. It is now ready to stuff. What you have removed would be far better saved for a coleslaw or bubble and squeak than added to the stuffing.

Final preparation
Heat the oven to 180°C/350°F/gas mark 4. Lightly oil a roasting tin or ovenproof dish. Spoon the stuffing into the vegetables and cover each with its own 'cap' if it has one. Stand all the vegetables upright in the oven dish or baking tin. Cover with foil to prevent them burning and cook in the centre/top of the oven. Cooking time will depend on the size of the vegetables and how much you have scooped out of the centre. The vegetables should be melting and tender, not *al dente*, so they will probably need to cook longer than you think. A firm cabbage can take a couple of hours; medium sized

onions could be done in little more than 40 minutes. Keep testing. Serve either from the dish in which they were cooked, or on a large earthenware platter in keeping with the rustic flavour and appearance of the dish.

Another variation
Stuffed vegetables are a tasty way of using up good quality leftovers. Cooked rice is the most usual filler, but sometimes, when I'm serving it, I often cook an extra portion of bulgur wheat (cracked wheat) so that I can use it the next day for stuffing onions or aubergines or whatever. Left-over lamb from a roast leg or best end served nice and pink combines with the bulgur wheat extremely well, as it would do with cooked rice. For an interesting texture I add some nuts and dried fruit. This mixture is also delicious for stuffing vine leaves. Incidentally, bulgur wheat is rich in fibre.

For each medium sized vegetable you need:

1 oz/25 g cooked lamb
2 oz/50 g cooked bulgur
   wheat
1 oz/25 g finely chopped
   onions
½ oz/15 g pine nuts or flaked
   almonds

½ oz/15 g raisins or chopped
   apricots
Pinch of mixed spice
Salt, pepper to taste
Olive oil, sufficient to moisten

Thoroughly mix all the ingredients and spoon into your chosen vegetables. Cook as above. I tend not to do tomatoes with other vegetables as they cook so much quicker. A dish of stuffed tomatoes on their own is delicious.

Stuffed
pancakes
MAKES 12

This once formed the main course of a Christmas dinner I cooked for vegetarian friends. I served the stuffed pancakes on a big earthenware platter and served the sauces in separate bowls. Many other fillings and sauces can be used for vegetarians and meat eaters alike.

6 oz/175 g wholemeal
   or 81%-flour
1 whole egg

1 egg yolk
⅔ pint/350 ml milk

Mix the batter by hand, in a blender or a processor. Let stand in a jug in a cool place for half an hour, then cook 12 pancakes in the usual way. Stack them up one on the other, cover with a tea-towel and leave to one side until you are ready to assemble them.

Sauce one
¾ lb / 350 g trimmed, washed and sliced leeks
¾ pint / 400 ml lightly salted water
½ oz / 15 g butter

Bring the water to the boil in a saucepan, drop in the leeks and simmer until soft. Put leeks into a blender or processor with a little of the cooking liquid. Process until very smooth, transfer to a bowl and beat in the butter to enrich and thicken the sauce. Set aside.

Sauce two
¾ lb / 350 g soft tomatoes
Half a chopped carrot
1 small chopped onion
½ oz / 15 g butter
¼ pint / 150 g *fromage frais*

Sweat the carrot and onion until fairly soft in a non-stick saucepan. Add the tomatoes and cook for about 20 minutes. Rub through a sieve into a bowl; beat in the butter and all the *fromage frais*. Season to taste and set to one side.

Sauce three
½ lb / 225 g whitest cup   Salt, pepper, nutmeg
   mushrooms, finely sliced   ½ pint / 300 ml smatana
½ oz / 15 g butter

Soften the mushrooms in the butter, add the smatana and simmer until flavourful and slightly reduced. Season to taste, and set aside.

Filling one
Gouda, Edam, Jarlsberg, St Paulin would be alternatives to the fontina.

6 oz / 175 g blanched and trimmed mangetouts
6 oz / 175 g fontina cheese

Filling two
½ teaspoon finely chopped fresh ginger
8 oz/225 g beansprouts, or other crunchy vegetable
A few sliced and fried mushrooms
A sprinkle of sherry or soy sauce

Filling three
8 oz/225 g cooked spinach or swiss chard
6 oz/175 g good blue cheese

Final preparation
Lightly oil your serving dish. Fill the first four pancakes with filling
no. 1 equally divided among them. Roll them and lay in one layer in
the oiled dish. Carry on with the next four pancakes, filling them
with the second mixture and so on, building up three layers of
stuffed pancakes. To finish, brush the top layer with olive oil and
sprinkle on the almonds or breadcrumbs and bake in a medium hot,
pre-heated oven for 15–20 minutes to make sure all the pancakes are
heated through and the various cheeses melted where appropriate.
  The crispest of salads should follow this rich, exotic dish.

Scrambled eggs with vegetables
SERVES 4

The real name of this dish is Eggs Casho, but I have changed it to a
more mundane though possibly more descriptive one, since few
people know our friend Steve Cash, a musician from Springfield,
Missouri, who claims to have invented the dish. He cooked it for us
one morning and served it with a bottle of 1969 Château Petrus that
had been left over from the previous evening. How we came to find
such a treasure and others like it in Springfield is another story for
another book. Eggs Casho is best made in a very large frying pan, or
perhaps even a wok. The ingredients can be varied, although eggs,
beansprouts and soy sauce are the essentials. A dish for breakfast,
lunch or supper.

1 tablespoon olive oil	3 oz/75 g mushrooms
2–3 oz/50–75 g celery	6 oz/175 g beansprouts
1 carrot	6 eggs
12 spring onions	Soy sauce

Heat the oil. Peel and trim the vegetables. Slice the celery on the oblique, shred the carrot, cut the spring onions into diagonal pieces and slice the mushrooms. Toss in the oil – celery first, then the carrots a minute or two later, then the onions, mushrooms and beansprouts. Beat the eggs with a teaspoon of soy sauce and pour over the vegetables. Turn with a spatula until just beginning to set. Serve immediately, with a little more soy sauce if liked. Cold, this makes a delicious filling for wholemeal rolls.

Potato and mushroom pie
SERVES 4
AMPLY

If you are lucky enough to find or buy wild mushrooms, cooking them with potatoes is a good way of making them go further, and the potatoes take on some of the mushroom flavour. You can moisten the mixture with olive oil, butter, cream or stock.

2 lb/900 g potatoes
Up to 1 lb/450 g mushrooms
½ lb/225 g onions

Seasoning
½ pint/300 ml stock

Scrub, peel and thinly slice the potatoes. Trim, wipe and slice the mushrooms. Peel and thinly slice the onions. Lightly oil an oven-proof dish or roasting pan and make alternate layers of potatoes, mushrooms and onion, finishing with a layer of potatoes. Season each layer, but lightly. Pour over the stock, cover with foil and bake in a moderate oven, 180°C/350°F/gas mark 4, for 45–60 minutes.

Potato and artichoke casserole
SERVES 4

This is a spring menu for when you can find those tiny, tender artichokes. When I've been on holiday in Italy or Gozo in the early part of the year, my luggage is largely made up of bags of vegetables; new potatoes, artichokes, lemons, fennel and real peas, not the modish mangetouts.

This recipe was described to me by Victor, a farmer friend in Gozo, after we had taken some time to establish that *articokks* (pronounced artichocks) were Jerusalem artichokes, whilst globe artichokes were, unpronounceably, *qaqoċċ*.

1 medium onion
Garlic cloves to taste
3 tablespoons fruity olive oil
1½ lb/675 g scrubbed new
  potatoes

4 small globe artichokes
3 ripe tomatoes, peeled, seeded
  and chopped
Seasoning

Peel and slice the onion and garlic and soften them in the olive oil in a heavy pan or casserole. Add the new potatoes and turn these until coated in oil. Wash and trim the artichokes down to the tender, edible leaves. Cut the base flat and stand the artichokes among the potatoes. Peel and slice the artichoke stalks if available and strew these over the vegetables. Do the same with the tomato. Season lightly, perhaps adding a bay leaf or sprig of marjoram. Cover with a lid or foil and cook until the vegetables are soft but not soggy.

This is a most versatile dish, and can be served as a starter or as a main course rather than as a vegetable accompaniment. Sometimes I have added a handful of fresh peas towards the end of the cooking time or a few small branches of broccoli. Red peppers go well with this too.

Braised fennel stuffed with cheese
SERVES 6

6 fennel bulbs, 4–5 oz/100–125 g each
3 shallots
2 oz/50 g goat cheese or blue cheese

2 oz/50 g Cheddar, Cantal or Edam
2 oz/50 g ricotta

Trim and clean the fennel and set aside any feathery tops. Cut the bulbs in half vertically. Remove enough of the centre to form a hollow big enough to hold a portion of stuffing. Chop the fennel removed from the centre into tiny dice. Peel and finely chop the shallots. Mix the fennel and shallots with the three cheeses, crumbling the blue cheese and grating the hard cheese.

Drop the fennel halves into a large pan of boiling water and cook them for 5–10 minutes. Remove and drain them. Divide the stuffing amongst the 6 fennel bulbs, fill the hollow and sandwich the two halves together. Tie them with thread and place them in a lightly oiled baking dish. Sprinkle with a few drops of water (or wine or stock or cider or lemon juice), cover with foil and place in a moderately hot oven, 190°C/375°F/gas mark 5, and cook for 15–20 minutes. Timing will depend on the age and freshness of the fennel. They may be done in less than 15 minutes, or take more than 20 if particularly tough and stringy.

This makes a very pleasing first course and if you have the oven on already, quite economical of fuel.

VEGETABLE SAUCES

When we stopped making flour-based sauces in the early 70s we had to look for some other agent to give the sauces body and substance. Double cream gave a good texture. A butter-mounted sauce really held, and is still, for me, one of the most satisfying creations in the kitchen. But it couldn't have done any good to add dollops of dairy fat every time you wanted to make a sauce. On a rare occasion perhaps, but generally speaking, the time had come to look at sauces in a different way altogether. The purpose of a sauce is not, after all, to mask the food but to heighten its qualities and complement its flavour.

Vegetable purées, those little dumps of baby food, had already become popular, and it did not take long to realise that in a slightly different form they made excellent sauces and soups. I have come across broccoli sauce and broad bean sauce which sound delicious; I have used a purée of tomato and beetroot left over from soup (see p. 26) as a sauce for pasta and for fish. Watercress sauce is excellent with just about everything and I don't know where we'd be without tomato *coulis*, both cooked and uncooked. But they do take a while to get right.

Three years ago I made a *coulis* of red peppers (capsicums) to go with a terrine of sweetbread. I wanted something bright and lively to offset the pale creamy looking terrine. I didn't want tomato and I didn't want anything very assertive to overwhelm the delicate flavours of the terrine. Red peppers seemed ideal. It was quite good, but not brilliant. It was when I tasted a truly brilliant version that I realised what I had done wrong. Gunther Schlender at the London restaurant Rue St. Jacques served a dish of simply cooked brill fillets arranged on a plate of three pepper sauces; red, green and yellow. Each sauce had its own distinctive flavour. It was Vincent Calcerano, the *maître d'hôtel*; who explained that the peppers had been roasted first. Of course. Obvious when you think about it. I had only steamed mine, hence the bland flavour.

Here, then, is a trio of my favourite vegetable sauces. Because they have no starch in them to hold them together, they separate, so pour on the sauce just before serving. Don't leave it sitting around on plates.

Incidentally, I wonder if the wheel will come full circle? Will we soon be serving a plate of, say, grilled *noisettes* of lamb sitting in a pool of smooth potato sauce?

Tomato coulis (uncooked)
MAKES ABOUT
1 pint/600 ml
SAUCE

The secret here is to cook the other ingredients but add the tomatoes just before you blend the sauce and before they have time to cook. Thus you have a wonderfully fresh-tasting sauce. The stock you use will depend on the sauce's final destination. Is it to go with fish or meat or pasta? The spices can be omitted for a less pronounced flavour.

1 tablespoon olive oil
2 shallots
½ stick celery
1 small carrot
2 cloves garlic
1 teaspoon chopped fresh or crystallised ginger

½ teaspoon cumin seeds
½ teaspoon coriander seeds
Seeds from 6 cardomom pods
¼ pint/150 ml stock
1 lb/450 g ripe tomatoes
Seasoning

Heat the olive oil in a heavy based pan and cook the peeled and chopped vegetables in it until lightly golden and soft. Do not let them turn much darker as they will give the sauce a bitter flavour if the slightest bit burnt. Stir in the spices and cook for a further 5 minutes. Add the stock and reduce by a third, 3–4 fl oz/100 ml. Roughly chop the tomatoes and put these in the bowl of a food processor or blender. Add the cooked vegetables, spices and stock. Process until smooth. Sieve. Season to taste and keep refrigerated until required if not needed immediately. It will keep for a couple of days.

Watercress sauce
MAKES
½ pint/300 ml
SAUCE

If you blanch the watercress leaves rather than cook them, the sauce will stay a clear bright green. The flavouring comes from the stalks. Parsley can be used in sauce in the same way, as can other herbs if you happen to have a glut of them.

2 big bunches watercress
3 shallots or 1 medium onion
¾ pint/450 ml stock

1 tablespoon thick yoghurt, *tofu* or *fromage frais*
Salt and pepper to taste

Trim the best green, leafy tops from the watercress, about half the total quantity, and put this to one side in a colander or sieve. Wash the rest and drain. Soften the shallots or onion in a little of the stock and then add the watercress stalks and coarser leaves. Cook these for about 10 minutes adding up to half the stock. Cool the mixture slightly and put it in the blender. Make a purée and pass it through a sieve into a basin. Pour boiling water over the best of the watercress to blanch it. Drain it and put it in the blender with the rest of the stock, the yoghurt, *tofu* or *fromage frais*. Make into a purée and stir it, without sieving into the first mixture. To heat it up again, put the basin over a pan of hot water. Serve hot but do not let it boil.

Pepper sauce
MAKES ½ pint/
300 ml SAUCE

Or capsicum sauce. The latter is more correct but is somehow not a comfortable description. Choose green, yellow or red peppers for whichever colour sauce you want. I have it on good authority from my friends at the restaurant Rue St. Jacques that the green pepper is most volatile in nature. You might be tempted to think, as I was, that the black peppers now available would make a stunning-looking sauce. I'm afraid not. Inside the flesh is quite, quite green.

12 oz/350 g peppers   ½ pint/300 ml stock
2 shallots   Seasoning

Char the peppers according to the instructions on p. 38. Remove every speck of skin. Peel the shallots and cut in quarters. Simmer in the stock with the peppers now cut into squares or strips. When soft, place the vegetables in the blender goblet. Reduce the stock by a third. Cool and pour into the blender. Blend until smooth and sieve, or not, as you prefer. Season to taste.

Like the other two sauces this can be served hot or cold.

Pasta, pulses and other Mediterranean dishes

For hundreds, if not thousands of years, the peoples of the Mediterranean shoreline have eaten a simple yet healthy diet in which the main elements are pasta, olive oil, wine, fish, fresh fruit and vegetables. Such a diet is well-balanced, far more so than the traditional Western diet with its concentration on meat, fat, processed foods and sugar. The Mediterranean diet with all its wonderful colours, aromas and flavours, straight from the sea, the fields or the cooking pot, has been described evocatively by Elizabeth David in *Mediterranean Food* and *Italian Food*; by Marcella Hazan in her wonderful books on Italian cuisine, where recipes and traditions are lovingly described; and most recently by Robin Howe in her book entitled simply *The Mediterranean Diet*. This is a fascinating book. Not a recipe book at all, but a description of what makes up the Mediterranean diet. Robin Howe has nevertheless given many ideas on the sort of dishes you might make at home. Her notes on the properties of good olive oil are particularly interesting and will persuade you to look for the best quality you can afford, if I have not been able to do so.

When I was in Liguria, I learned, from the same source as Robin Howe, of a new way of cooking dried pasta. Eva Agnesi, president of one of Italy's largest pasta manufacturers where they mill their own durum wheat, explained that you bring the water to the boil, put in more than 100 g/a scant 4 oz pasta per person, boil it uncovered for 2 minutes if it's thin pasta, 3 minutes if thick. Then you turn the heat off, cover the pan with a tight-fitting lid and allow it to stand for the full cooking time stated on the packet. In this way you conserve energy and also lose fewer of the nutrients into the water. Drain and serve in the usual way. The very best dried pasta I have found here is made from durum wheat with the wheatgerm put back into the dough. It contains 16% protein, a considerably higher proportion than most others on the market. Called Gemma, it is manufactured by Agnesi and is available in a number of Italian delicatessens. I cook it in the way described above and try to resist the temptation to serve more than 4 oz/100 g per person. Pasta is not fattening. It is only fattening if you eat it in large quantities and/or with rich buttery, creamy, meaty sauces. A little olive oil and herbs are perfect, as is a light sauce made from lightly cooked and puréed vegetables.

Whilst you can now get very good fresh pasta in many places, it is still worth making your own because you can vary the fillings beyond the usual spinach and ricotta or veal and chicken. If you have a food processor and a handcranked or an electric pasta maker, you will be able to use a proportion of fine semolina (milled from durum wheat) in your mixture. This is difficult to do if you are making the dough entirely by hand.

I have given only one risotto recipe, but from this you can make a number of variations. One of the most delicious risottos I know is arborio rice cooked with stock according to the method given on p. 70, finished with a little butter and freshly grated Parmesan cheese. A simple *risotto bianco*.

Other excellent grain dishes can be made from bulgur wheat, also known as cracked wheat and burghul, and from *couscous* which is made from millet and a staple in the North African countries bordering the Mediterranean. This latter can be made into a splendid party dish for an unusual, informal dinner. Using the basic recipe on p. 70 you can cook an assortment of meats, lamb kebabs, meatballs, spicy sausages, chicken joints and arrange these on a large platter of steamed *couscous*. With this serve a large pot of fragrant vegetable stew and a small bowl of hot pepper sauce. Before, serve some small appetisers – olives, hard boiled eggs (quail eggs if you can get them) toasted almonds, stuffed vine leaves. Hand round flat, unleavened bread and encourage everyone to eat with their fingers for true authenticity. Finger bowls with a mixture of water and rosewater can be near to hand. Finish the meal with sliced oranges sprinkled with orange flower water, garnished with fresh mint. A Moroccan feast.

Beans of all kinds figure largely in the cuisine of the Mediterranean area and we are lucky enough to be able to buy many varieties of this cheap and delicious source of protein.

Pasta, rice and beans should be seen as the delicious vehicle for serving small quantities of meat or fish protein. Their main attraction is that they taste and smell so good and are so versatile and challenging to the cook.

Fusilli with basil, broad beans and tomatoes
SERVES 4

This is one of the summeriest pasta dishes I know. The vegetables are hardly cooked at all, except by the hot pasta. Fusilli hold a chunky sauce like this well. Or you might like to serve home-made tagliatelle or, even better, pappardelle (quite broad, short strips of pasta) which seems to fold itself around a sauce in a way that tagliatelle cannot do.

1½ lb/675 g broad beans	Few sprigs of basil
1 lb/450 g ripe tomatoes	Salt, pepper, crushed garlic to
1 lb/450 g pasta	taste
2–3 tablespoons olive oil	

Shell the broad beans and put them into a deep sieve or steamer basket. Peel, seed and chop the tomatoes. Bring a large pan of water to the boil, salt it or not, and drop in the pasta. When it is almost cooked (and the cooking time will depend on whether it is fresh or dried) place the sieve or basket of beans in the water for a couple of minutes. Remove the beans. Drain the pasta. Toss it in olive oil and add the beans, the chopped tomatoes and basil leaves shredded by hand. Season to taste with salt, pepper and garlic. Enjoy the fresh flavours of this dish without adding cheese.

Pasta with walnut sauce

This sauce is prepared in a similar way to *pesto*, the fragrant basil and olive oil mixture from Liguria. Towards the end of the summer I pick as many basil leaves as I can and make up a few small pots of *pesto* to keep in the fridge, but once it's gone I can never bring myself to buy the bottled versions, some of them very good. Instead I like to make up a walnut and parsley mixture which is particularly good when made with flat leaf parsley. If I'm planning to keep the sauce for a few weeks, I make it without garlic which I find turns things rancid after a while.

Cook your pasta according to whether it is fresh, dry or home-made and serve with it some of the following sauce. The quantities given will fill four 4 oz/100 g jars. A food processor is very useful for this recipe.

3 oz/75 g flat leaf parsley
6 oz/175 g freshly shelled
  walnuts
4 oz/100 g freshly grated
  Parmesan

6 tablespoons olive oil or
  walnut oil

Strip the leaves from the parsley and chop them up in the food processor. Add the walnuts and Parmesan. Process for 30 seconds and then gradually add the oil. When thoroughly blended, pack into small jars, cover with clingfilm and secure with rubber bands. The sauce will keep for 6–8 weeks in the refrigerator. It is one of the things I like to give as small gifts; makes a change from home-made jam.

14 oz/400 g mixed orange,
  green and white fusilli
1 tablespoon extra virgin olive
  oil
4 oz/125 g fine haricot beans,
  green beans or small
  mangetouts
4 oz/125 g white button
  mushrooms

4 ripe but firm tomatoes
2 cloves garlic, crushed
5 fl oz/150 ml vegetable or
  chicken stock
Chopped fresh herbs

*Fusilli
tricolore*
SERVES 4

First make the vegetable sauce for the pasta. Heat the olive oil in a heavy based saucepan or frying pan. Top and tail the beans or mangetouts. Snap the beans in three or four places depending on length, keeping the mangetouts whole. Wipe and quarter or slice the mushrooms. Peel, deseed and cut the tomato into strips about $\frac{1}{4}$ in/$\frac{1}{2}$ cm wide. Stir the beans or mangetouts in the hot oil and cook for 3 or 4 minutes, add the mushroom and tomatoes and cook for 2 minutes more. Stir in the crushed garlic and the stock. Allow to bubble quite fiercely so that the stock and oil emulsify and thicken. Meanwhile cook the pasta in plenty of lightly salted water according to the directions, usually a minute or so for fresh shop-bought pasta and 8–10 minutes for dried. Drain the pasta, sprinkle on a few drops more oil and stir in the vegetables. Serve in heated shallow soup plates and sprinkle with fresh herbs.

Spaghetti with sunflower seeds
SERVES 4

This is an excellent standby dish in that the sauce can be made from the contents of a judiciously stocked store cupboard and enlivened with whatever fresh herbs you can find. When I first made this dish it was the end of an Indian summer and, unusually for October, fresh basil was still around and abundant.

14 oz/400 g dried spaghetti	2 crushed cloves garlic
2 oz/50 g sunflower seeds	Black pepper
1 oz/25 g sun-dried tomato paste	Olive oil to taste

Cook the spaghetti as described on p. 56 or according to the instructions on the packet. Meanwhile toast the sunflower seeds until quite brown, but not burnt. I prefer to do this in a large non-stick frying pan. Stir in the tomato paste, garlic and pepper. Add a little olive oil, and salt if necessary. Drain the pasta when cooked, turn it in the sauce in the frying pan, adding more oil if you wish. Tip into a warmed serving bowl and serve immediately.

Tagliatelle with vodka and salmon
SERVES 4

The two main ingredients of the sauce for this recipe have little to do with the Mediterranean or indeed, Italy, but it is a dish which appears frequently on restaurant menus. It could hardly be described as healthy, but it is quite, quite delicious and is a nice way of serving salmon at the beginning of the season when it is very expensive. Don't cook the salmon first; stirring it into the hot pasta cooks it quite enough. For this dish I like to use fresh pasta.

14 oz/400 g fresh tagliatelle	Freshly ground black pepper
8 oz/225 g salmon fillet	1 oz/25 ml vodka
3 oz/75 g *crème fraîche* or rich Greek yoghurt	1 oz/25 g butter

While bringing the water to the boil for the pasta, skin the salmon fillet and cut it into the thinnest slivers. Beat up the cream or yoghurt with a little black pepper and the vodka. Put the tagliatelle into boiling water. Cook until *al dente*, drain and toss immediately in butter. Add the salmon pieces and mix thoroughly with the pasta. Stir in the cream and vodka mixture and turn until the pasta is well coated. Serve immediately, letting each person add salt to taste. Quarters of lemon might also be passed with this dish.

Pasta with radicchio and olives
SERVES 4

One winter we were in Trieste and noticed signs and pictures in all the restaurant and food shop windows of Treviso lettuce, *radicchio*. It was clearly the beginning of the season for this bitter, tightly curled red lettuce. Here we tend to serve it just as part of a rather superior salad. (It is expensive in England, but I find it keeps better than many of the green lettuces and so is reasonably economical.) In Trieste it was served as a cooked vegetable. So once back in my kitchen, I began to experiment. Unfortunately it does seem to lose its deep red colour in cooking, so it is no use thinking of it in terms of what colour it might add to a dish. The distinctive nutty, bitter flavour stays on however. Best of all I like it quickly tossed into a dish of pasta.

14 oz/400 g dried or fresh spaghetti or tagliatelle
2 tablespoons olive oil
4 oz/100–125 g olives

4–6 oz/125–150 g *radicchio*
1 crushed clove garlic
Freshly ground black pepper

Cook the pasta in very lightly salted water. Heat the olive oil in a pan. Stone and roughly chop the olives. This makes them cling to the sauce better. Shred the washed *radicchio* by hand and stir into the oil. Add the garlic. Drain the pasta, stir it into the oil and olive mixture until well coated and then serve in a warm serving bowl. Grind on some black pepper.

Pasta with sardines
SERVES 4

We first ate this marvellous Sicilian speciality at the excellent Charleston restaurant in Palermo. As he drove us in from the airport the night before, our taxi driver claimed that it was no longer possible to get a good dish of *pasta con le sarde* in any restaurant, but he wasn't too bothered since his wife made the very best in the world. So it was more in the spirit of gastronomic research than in eager anticipation of a long awaited treat that we ordered a dish for lunch. It was quite extraordinarily good. What kind of genius was Signora taxi driver, I wondered, if she could produce better than this? The sardines made the dish rich, the capers gave it a piquancy, the raisins a sweetness, and the whole was redolent of fennel, particularly the feathery tops which are snapped off and, seemingly, discarded when you buy fennel in the winding market at the back of the main street in Palermo. Seemingly, I write advisedly, since I do wonder whether the bundles of feathery fronds don't finish up in the restaurant kitchens of Palermo.

I have cooked the dish at home with some success. But best of all would be to grow your own fennel and charcoal grill the sardines out in the garden. I have no charcoal grill and can never get enough fennel tops on the mutilated stumps we buy in the shops.

4 good sized sardines or 8 small ones	1 oz/25 g raisins
	1 oz/25 g pine nuts
1 medium fennel bulb	1–2 cloves garlic
1 shallot or small onion	Seasoning
1 tablespoon olive oil	14 oz/400 g dried pasta
1 oz/25 g capers	(spaghetti or buccatini)

Clean and scale the sardines. Remove the feathery tops from the fennel and put these to one side. Finely chop the fennel and shallot and sweat it in the olive oil. When these are soft, add the capers, raisins, pine nuts and crushed garlic. Season lightly with salt and pepper. Cook together gently, moistening if necessary with a little more oil, water or a spot of white wine.

While the sauce is cooking, grill the sardines under a hot grill and cook the pasta in plenty of boiling water according to the directions on the packet, or follow the method on p. 56. At this stage, chop up whatever you have in the way of fennel tops and add this to the sauce. Drain the pasta, toss it in olive oil and then in the fennel sauce. Pour it into a heated serving bowl. Working quickly, fillet the sardines and lay on top of the dish of pasta. Serve immediately.

Another wonderfully easy and quickly prepared pasta dish. Ideally, it should be made in the summer when you can find the freshest, sweetest garden peas. Bottled *petits pois* from France or Belgium make a useful alternative if you have to have peas, but if they are not available why not use another sort of fresh vegetable – broccoli florets, or fine slices of celery or fennel?

Pasta with mushrooms and peas
SERVES 4

8 oz/225 g fresh mushrooms
4 oz/125 g fresh peas, shelled
  weight
1 lb/450 g pasta
3 tablespoons olive oil

Few sprigs of parsley, chervil
  or summer savory
Salt, pepper, crushed garlic to
  taste

Wipe the mushrooms, peeling them only if absolutely necessary, and slice them. Put them, together with the peas in a sieve or steamer basket. Bring a large pan of water to the boil, salt it or not, and drop in the pasta. When it is almost cooked, place the basket of mushrooms and peas in the steam for a couple of minutes. Remove the basket and drain the pasta. Toss it in olive oil and add the peas, mushrooms, herbs and seasoning.

I have been lucky enough to find the small clams called Venus regularly in a London fishmonger's and like to serve them, still in their shells or half shell, with pasta. Mussels are equally good served in this way.

Pasta with clams
SERVES 4

4 lb/1.80 kg Venus clams or
  mussels
1 bunch spring onions
12 oz/350 g ripe tomatoes,
  peeled and seeded

2 tablespoons olive oil
1 lb/450 g pasta
Seasoning

Scrub the shellfish, discarding any that are open. Rinse them thoroughly. Place them in a large, lidded saucepan over a high heat and steam for 2–3 minutes until they open. Meanwhile, trim the spring onions and slice them into fine rings. Roughly chop the tomatoes. Gently stew both vegetables in the olive oil, using a large frying pan. Cook the pasta according to whether it is fresh or dried. Strain the cooking juices from the shellfish on to the vegetables and reduce slightly. Leave the clams or mussels attached to the half shell and discard the other half. Drain the pasta, turn it in the sauce, season to taste and pour it into a heated bowl. Add the shellfish and serve immediately.

Parcels of pasta with scallops

SERVES 4

For the pasta
7 oz/200 g strong white flour
2 size-3 eggs

You can make the dough very easily if you have a food processor. Put the flour into the bowl, add the two eggs and process, in short bursts, for 30 seconds. The texture will be crumbly but soft. Scoop it all together and form it into a ball. Let it rest covered in clingfilm in a cool place for 10–15 minutes. If you make the dough by hand, heap the flour on to a marble slab or your usual surface for making pastry. Make a well in the centre of the flour and slide in the two eggs. Work into a dough with your fingertips and form it into a ball. Let it rest covered in clingfilm in a cool place for 10–15 minutes.

Cut off a piece the size of an egg and roll it out as thinly as possible, no thicker than a 20p piece if possible. I find it easier to work with small pieces of dough although of course *real* pasta makers work with large quantities and still manage to roll it out thinly, using their hands to stretch the dough as they go. When you have a sheet of thin pasta, stamp out circles with a pastry cutter, 2–4 in/5–10 cm in diameter. The size is not particularly important – if you cut out large ones, you'll probably only want two per serving, four or five if small. Place the pasta rounds in a single layer, and not touching, on a board or tray covered with a clean tea-towel, and cover them with a barely damp tea-towel while you prepare the filling and the sauce.

For the filling and the sauce

8 large scallops with good big corals
7 fl oz/200 ml fish stock
2 tablespoons finely chopped shallots
Seasoning

Pinch of saffron threads
½ oz/15 g unsalted butter (or a non-stick frying pan)
Fresh coriander, basil, chervil or parsley for garnish

Prepare the scallops by separating the coral from the white part. Remove the thin, dark intestine which encircles the scallop and the small cushion of muscle which toughens during cooking if not removed. Wash quickly to remove any sand and dry thoroughly.

Slice six of the scallops into two or three rounds and chop the remaining two into tiny pieces.

Heat the fish stock in a pan. Put three tablespoons of it into a bowl or teacup and in it steep the saffron threads. Boil the chopped shallot in the remaining stock until soft. Strain the stock and reserve the shallots.

To make the stuffing for the pasta, chop the coral on a board until you have a thick paste. Mix in the shallots and the chopped white scallop meat. Lightly season with freshly ground white pepper and the merest hint of salt.

Uncover the pasta circles. Taking them one by one, spoon a small amount of stuffing into each (a coffee spoon or a teaspoon, depending on the size of the pasta). Dampen the edges, fold over and seal into a half-moon shape. Return to the covered tray until required. You can prepare up to this point several hours in advance. I usually do these in the afternoon before a dinner party. It is not something to be left until the last minute.

To finish the dish, bring a large pan of lightly salted boiling water to the boil, to which you add a drop or two of oil to prevent the pasta from sticking together. Meanwhile, heat the butter in a frying pan or heat a non-stick frying pan and quickly fry the scallops on both sides, 30 seconds is all that is required. Remove and keep in a warm place. Add the stock and the saffron liquid to the frying pan. Allow to boil quite fiercely and reduce by a third. You want to be left with about 6 tablespoons of sauce.

Drop the pasta parcels into the boiling water. Bring back to the boil and cook for 2–3 minutes until just tender. Length of time depends on how quickly or thinly you rolled your pasta. Drain. Place a spoonful of sauce on each heated serving plate and on it some of the pasta parcels. Around them arrange two or three pieces of scallop and garnish with fresh herbs.

Tortellini with goat's cheese and walnuts

SERVES 4 AS A STARTER, 2 AS A MAIN COURSE

Pasta that you've made yourself is one of the nicest dishes to serve friends. Infinitely versatile, it lends itself to unusual or simple fillings. Ricotta is often used, but here I use goat's cheese for a slightly more distinctive flavour. Walnuts, crushed with garlic complete the ingredients for the filling.

For the pasta

5 oz/150 g strong white flour   2 size-3 eggs
2 oz/50 g fine semolina

Heap up the dry ingredients and make a well in the top. Slide in the two eggs and work in the flour, gradually, with the fingertips, until thoroughly mixed. Then knead to a smooth dough, working on a floured board. Break off a piece of dough and roll out to the thickness of a 20p piece. Cut into rounds with a pastry cutter. Place a small amount of filling in the centre, wet the edges, fold over and seal. Continue until the dough and the filling are used up.

For the filling

4 oz/100 g goat's cheese	2 cloves garlic
2 oz/50 g walnuts	Black pepper ·

Remove the rind from the goat's cheese. Pound the walnuts and peeled garlic and mix with the cheese. Season to taste with black pepper.

Cook the stuffed pasta in plenty of boiling water, salted or not, according to your preference. Drain and serve with a little olive oil and a sprinkling of freshly grated nutmeg and chopped chives.

Hot pear and Stilton ravioli
SERVES 4 AS A STARTER

My mother-in-law once described to me how her Russian mother used to make exquisite noodle dough by first making a batch of creamy mashed potatoes, beating in plenty of butter and then adding to it as much flour as it would take to make a firm but pliable dough. That night, I dreamt about a hot, sweet pudding with the same sort of dough. In the dream I sweetened the dough with honey, rolled it out, stamped it into circles and filled it with sliced fresh strawberries before sealing it and placing the ravioli gently into hot water.

I'm not at all sure that cooked strawberries are a good idea and have never made the dish of my dreams. Pears or apples and flavoursome cheese prepared in this way make an unusual starter however, or a combined pudding and savoury course. As a starter, I would, I think, leave out the honey.

8 oz/225 g freshly mashed potatoes	3 oz/75 g strong white flour
2 oz/50 g salted butter	2 ripe pears
Seasoning	4 oz/100 g blue Stilton or other tasty cheese
2 tablespoons milk	

Make the dough by first beating the butter, milk and seasoning into the mashed potatoes. Then add the flour. You may need more or less than the recipe states, depending on how moist your potatoes are in the first place.

Let the dough rest, covered, for 20 minutes. Break off egg-sized pieces and roll out either by hand or in a pasta machine to no more than the thickness of a 10p piece. Peel, core and chop the fruit. Cut up or grate the cheese. Cut the dough into circles or other shapes. Put a teaspoon of cheese and fruit in the centre. Wet the edges of the dough, fold over and seal. Set aside on a board covered with a tea-towel and continue until you have used up all the dough and filling. Any left-over dough can be rolled out, cut into narrow strips, allowed to dry for use in soup another day. Bring a large pan of water to the boil and slide in the ravioli. After 3–4 minutes remove with a slotted spoon and serve immediately sprinkled with a little olive oil and fresh parsley.

Spinach gnocchi

SERVES 4 AS A STARTER, 2 AS A MAIN COURSE

This recipe was arrived at somewhat by trial and error, like most I suppose. *Gnocchi* are difficult to handle because the mixture is so soft and sticky, and although not authentic, I do find half a beaten egg helps to hold it together. The main reason *gnocchi* break up is that the water is boiling too fiercely when they are dropped in. The surface of the water should scarcely break.

5–6 oz/150–175 g mashed
  potatoes
3 oz/75 g semolina
4 oz/125 g finely chopped,
  cooked spinach
4 oz/125 g ricotta
1 oz/25 g freshly grated
  Parmesan

½ beaten egg
1 teaspoon salt
Ground white pepper
Plenty of freshly ground
  nutmeg

Mix the ingredients quickly but thoroughly together, but avoid handling too much. Take about a teaspoonful of the mixture, roll it into a ball and then roll it along the prongs of a fork to groove it. Set aside on a tea-towel until you have used up all the mixture. Bring a large pan of lightly salted water to the boil. Lower a few *gnocchi* at a time into the barely simmering water. They will sink to the bottom. When cooked they will rise to the top and float. Remove with a slotted spoon, drain and place in a buttered or oiled ovenproof dish. Proceed with the rest of the mixture, cooking the *gnocchi* in batches. Dot them with butter and sprinkle on Parmesan. Heat through in the oven or under the grill.

Another variation, which is delicious with home-made tomato sauce, uses no spinach but increases the proportion of ricotta to 6 oz/175 g and the Parmesan to 3 oz/75 g.

Bread and tomatoes

This simplest of all dishes is one of my very favourite Mediterranean treats. I have enjoyed it in Liguria where it was made special by the wonderfully fruity, light oil of the region, in Valencia as *pan catalan* where the misshapen, ripe outdoor tomatoes gave it a special flavour, but best of all in Gozo where the bread is justly famous and the garlic so green, fresh and piquant you can eat it as you would spring onions. Like so many simple dishes the secret lies in the quality of the ingredients. What you need is bread, olive oil, tomatoes, garlic, salt and pepper in whatever quantities and proportions you think fitting. Slice the bread thickly. Drizzle on plenty of olive oil. Roughly chop the tomatoes and spread them on top of the bread. Crush the garlic in a little salt and distribute this amongst the tomato pulp. Sprinkle on a little freshly ground black pepper. If you can possibly bear it, let this stand in a cool place for 10–15 minutes to let the flavours mingle. It is only a little less delicious when eaten immediately.

Clafoutis provençale
MAKES 12
SMALL
CLAFOUTIS
OR A
SINGLE ONE
8 IN/20 CM
IN DIAMETER

I have adapted this dish from the Limousin *clafoutis* which is, traditionally, cherries baked in a batter and served as a pudding. Mine is a savoury recipe and can be used to make up a substantial first course or to make miniature *clafoutis* to serve as snacks or as savouries at the end of a meal. It is a remarkably versatile mixture, both as a savoury and a sweet. Herbs, cheese or cooked diced vegetables can be added to the batter, as can sweet things, such as candied fruit or chopped almonds and raisins. You can use strong flour, stoneground, wholewheat etc. according to taste.

1 heaped tablespoon flour
1 size-3 egg
¼ pint/150 ml milk or milk
   and water mixed
2 tomatoes

2 oz/50 g black olives
1 clove garlic crushed –
   optional
6 anchovy fillets

First beat the flour, egg and liquid together to make a smooth batter. Let it stand for at least half an hour. Peel, de-seed and dice the tomatoes. Remove the stones from the olives and chop them and mix with the tomato and garlic. Lightly oil a flan dish or bun tin, or use non-stick baking equipment. Put a teaspoonful of mixed tomato, olive and garlic in each tin, or spread the whole over the base of a flan dish. Snip up the anchovy fillets and sprinkle these on top. Pour on the batter and bake in a pre-heated oven, 200°C/400°F/gas mark 6, for 30–35 minutes. They should be quite dark golden brown and puffed up when cooked, though will sink somewhat when removed from the oven. Serve warm.

Bulgur wheat salad

SERVES 4

This makes a substantial and colourful first course. I use a measuring jug since it is a question of volume rather than weight in this recipe.

1 pint/600 ml water or stock
½ pint/300 ml bulgur wheat
Olive oil
Spring onions or chives
Black olives
Peeled, seeded and chopped
   tomatoes

Fresh mint
Fresh coriander
Garlic
Seasoning

Bring the water or stock to the boil. Pour in the bulgur wheat and remove from the heat. Allow to stand for 5 minutes or so by which time the liquid will all be absorbed. Stir occasionally to break up any lumps. Pour the cooked wheat into a large serving bowl and allow it to cool before you add the other ingredients otherwise it will tend to cook them.

   This salad is best served just tepid rather than from the refrigerator. You could add hard boiled eggs and perhaps a little left-over grilled meat or fish, and turn this into a main course for lunch or supper.

Bean and
pasta soup
SERVES 4

This is a particularly delicious and satisfying soup. (The combination of the grain in the pasta and the pulse provides first class protein.) It is a good way of using up cooked beans from another dish, but is well worth making from scratch too. Haricot or cannellini beans are good in soup.

1 tablespoon olive oil	8 oz/225 g cooked beans
1 onion, peeled and chopped or sliced	2 pints/1.2 ml stock
2 cloves garlic, crushed	2 oz/50 g dried pasta
4 ripe tomatoes, peeled, with the seeds removed	1 dessertspoon *pesto* – optional

Cook the onion, garlic and tomato in the olive oil for a few minutes. Pour on the stock, bring to the boil and reduce by about 10 fl oz/ 300 ml. Pour a little liquid into the blender, add 2 oz/50 g of the beans and make a purée. Add this and the rest of the beans to the stock and bring back to the boil. Add the pasta and cook until it is *al dente*. Season to taste and stir in the *pesto* if you have it. It does add a lovely flavour to these rich robust soups.

This soup can be made in many versions, adding courgettes, turnip, watercress, celery to turn it into a meal in itself, to be accompanied by good crusty bread, a glass of wine and some fresh fruit to follow.

Pumpkin
risotto
SERVES 4

I particularly like this soothing, golden dish. Cristallo or arborio rice are the ones traditionally used for risotto. You can use brown rice, but it will not have quite the same creaminess. Mushrooms or other ingredients can be substituted for the pumpkin.

8 oz/225 g piece fresh pumpkin	2 pints/1.2 litres stock
1 tablespoon olive oil	11 oz/300 g rice
2 shallots or 1 medium onion, finely chopped	1 oz/25 g butter

First prepare the pumpkin, removing the rind. Shred and leave in a bowl of water to which you've added a drop or two of vinegar or lemon juice and a pinch of salt.

Heat the oil in a heavy pan or casserole. Cook the shallots or onions in it until soft and transparent. Add the thoroughly drained pumpkin. Meanwhile heat the stock. Stir the rice into the vegetables until coated with oil, taking care not to burn it. Turn up the heat and add ¼ pint/150 ml stock and stir. When this is almost absorbed, add the same quantity of stock again, stirring continuously. Carry on until you have about ¼ pint/150 ml of stock left by which time the rice will be almost cooked, creamy all the way through, and the pumpkin tender. You may not need to add any more stock, but stir in the butter and serve immediately.

A version of minestrone soup was one of the first things I learned to cook, when I was about eleven. Bacon rinds and trimmings provided the flavouring. Now, if I can, I make my stock with a knuckle bone from a Parma ham. The soup is even better the next day and, again, almost makes a meal in itself. It should be so full of beans and vegetables that a spoon will practically stand up in it. The beans to use are haricot, cannellini or, best of all, the pinkish borlotti beans.

Minestrone, cooked in a clay pot
SERVES 6–8

8 oz/225 g soaked beans	Cloves of garlic, to taste
1 tablespoon olive oil	2½ pints/1.5 litres stock
1 onion	4 oz/100 g shredded cabbage
1 carrot	2 oz/50 g green beans or
1 stick celery	courgettes
1 leek	Seasoning
1 small white turnip	1 tablespoon *pesto*, optional
2 or 3 ripe tomatoes	

Soak your clay pot in cold water for 15 minutes. Place the soaked beans in the bottom half. Heat the olive oil in a frying pan. Peel and finely chop the vegetables, removing the seeds from the tomatoes. Turn these in the olive oil and, when lightly browned, add them to the beans. Bring the stock to the boil and pour it over the vegetables. Cover with the lid and cook in a low oven, 170°C/325°F/gas mark 3, for 2–3 hours. About half an hour before the end, add the cabbage and beans or courgettes. Season to taste and allow to cook until the green vegetables are just done. To serve, stir in a little *pesto* or a little more olive oil.

The meat for a *couscous* is traditionally grilled or fried, but there is no reason why it should not be steamed – it is healthy and economical of fuel, since it can be cooked on top of the rest of the

Chicken couscous
SERVES 4

meal. The recipe can be varied by substituting lamb fillet, cut into chunks, or spicy sausages, both of which should be grilled.

1½ pints/900 ml chicken stock
6 oz/175 g chick peas, soaked for 12 hours
2 small white turnips
3 carrots
3 courgettes
1 green or red pepper
2 leeks
1 teaspoon cumin seeds
1 teaspoon coriander seeds

1–2 tablespoons chopped coriander leaves
Salt and pepper
1 tin or tube of *harissa* (hot chilli paste)
4 chicken breasts
12 oz/350 g *couscous*
2 tablespoons raisins
1 tablespoon flaked almonds

If you cannot buy *harissa*, a hot purée of peppers usually sold in small tins or tubes, mix 1 tablespoon of paprika with half a teaspoon of cayenne pepper and moisten with a little oil to make a paste.

Put the stock in a large pan or *couscoussier*. Wash, peel, dice, slice and chop the vegetables as appropriate. Add these, with a pinch of cumin and coriander and a touch of *harissa* to the stock. Bring to the boil and simmer gently for 30–40 minutes. The vegetables in a *couscous* are generally served well cooked rather than *al dente*, with most of the flavour in the sauce.

Prepare the chicken breasts by removing any skin and bone. Crush the rest of the cumin and coriander and mix it with the chopped fresh coriander and a little salt and pepper. Coat the chicken with this mixture and place in a steamer basket set over the vegetables. Steam gently, covered. Meanwhile prepare the *couscous* by tipping it on to a plate. Moisten it with warm water. Mix with your fingers to break up any lumps. After 5 minutes or so, moisten a little more. Then put the *couscous* in a steamer basket, or in the top of the *couscoussier* and let it steam for 10 minutes, by which time the chicken should also be cooked.

To serve, place a pot of the vegetable soup on the table, with a small bowl of *harissa*. Spread the *couscous* on a large platter, garnish with raisins and almonds and arrange the chicken pieces on top.

Fish and shellfish

For all sorts of reasons, fish is one of my favourite foods. To begin with, it is simply delicious and can be deliciously simple. Its fine delicate texture requires only a little careful cooking; overcooking spoils it horribly. At its best and freshest it can be delicious raw, served as *sushi* or *sashimi* in the Japanese fashion. It lends itself to quick and easy cooking methods, grilling, poaching, steaming or cooking in a non-stick frying pan, all of which, incidentally are extremely healthy ways of cooking. Thus it would be a pity to smother such delicate light dishes with rich creamy sauces, full of butter, brandy and cream, delicious though these might be on occasion. No, for this fish cookery, I like simple sauces best: reduced cooking liquors or marinades, purées of herbs, sorrel, watercress or tomatoes. Cream substitutes such as yoghurt or *tofu* can be used to thicken or enrich those sauces that require it, but I prefer to keep it light and simple so that the taste of the fish comes through.

Fish is so varied in its flavours and textures, far more so than meat, I think. A fillet of sole is rich and densely textured yet smooth, with quite a different flavour from turbot, which is itself quite different from sea-bass. Monkfish is a robust fish which lends itself to many different cooking methods, some more akin to the way in which you might prepare meat. Mackerel and other oily fish can take stronger flavours, such as the gooseberry sauce traditionally served with mackerel. Even within the large cod family there is a difference between cod and haddock; and whiting, particularly delicate and liable to break up easily, is invaluable as a basis for mousses and terrines. All this variety without even mentioning freshwater fish, shellfish, crustaceans and the whole range of smoked fish.

More and more we are being exhorted to buy fish, to get to know our fishmongers, to seek his or her advice. This is not before time. It was worrying to see wet fish shops closing down. Fish is and always has been one of our greatest natural resources. That it is delicious and healthy as well is a bonus. That it is a minority taste in Britain is a puzzle.

Buried mackerel
SERVES 4

A version of the ubiquitous *gravad lax*. The malic acid content of apple juice makes it an extremely good and effective marinade ingredient. The flavouring is coriander, one of my favourites, and one which goes well with fish. The mackerel should be carefully filleted with all the bones removed.

1 large mackerel	1 teaspoon sugar
1 tablespoon coarse sea salt	2 tablespoons finely chopped
1 tablespoon crushed	coriander leaves
coriander seeds	4–6 tablespoons apple juice

Place one of the fillets in a shallow dish. Mix the salt, coriander seeds, sugar and coriander leaves. Spread this over the mackerel fillet, sprinkle on some of the apple juice and place the other fillet on top. Spoon the rest of the apple juice over the fish. Cover with clingfilm and place a weighted board or plate on top (cartons of fruit juice or milk make good weights). Place in the fridge for 12–24 hours.

To serve, slice the fish diagonally into thin slices and serve on individual plates with a small salad of thin apple slices, using both red and green apples for contrast, onion rings and a sprig or two of coriander leaves. Dress the salad with a little apple juice flavoured with a spot of sesame oil and sprinkle toasted sesame seeds over it.

Oriental salad with fresh tuna fish
SERVES 4

Thinly sliced fish cooked quickly and served warm on cool salad leaves is something I am particularly fond of as a starter. Occasionally we can get tuna fish which I like to prepare this way; otherwise we have a fairly firm-fleshed fish. Salmon is delicious, and thin slices from a mackerel fillet are surprisingly delicate and go well with the exotic flavours in the dressing.

I like to add nuts or seeds to such a salad and match it to the oil used; hazelnuts and hazelnut oil, walnuts and walnut oil, toasted sunflower seeds and sunflower oil and, perhaps best of all for an authentic oriental flavour, toasted sesame seeds with sesame oil. Be warned though, the latter is very strong. You might prefer to blend it with a little sunflower or grapeseed oil. (Here I blend 1 teaspoon with 1½ tablespoons sunflower oil.) The small quantity of fruit is important to balance the flavours. Peach, mango, grapes, lychees, apples are all appropriate as, I am sure, are other fruits which you will discover on experimenting.

Some or all of the following gives enough for 4 people:

Chinese leaves	2 tablespoons mixed sunflower
Lettuce	and sesame oil, plus
Endive	1 teaspoon extra of the
Watercress	mixture
1 leek or 3 spring onions	1 teaspoon lime or lemon juice
3 oz/75 g beansprouts	or rice vinegar
2 oz/50 g fruit	8 oz/225 g fresh tuna fish (or
2 cloves garlic	salmon)
1 teaspoon soy sauce	1 tablespoon toasted sesame
	seeds

Pick over, wash and dry the salad leaves carefully. Arrange on individual serving plates. Large ones are best. Wash, trim and shred the leek or spring onions. Mix with the beansprouts. Prepare the fruit as appropriate. Apple should be finely sliced, grapes peeled and halved, mango peeled and cut into *julienne* strips etc. Mix with the sprouts and onion. Crush the garlic and mix well with the soy sauce, oil and lime juice. Toss the beansprouts etc. in this and let stand in a basin while you prepare the fish. Slice the fish as thinly as possible. Heat a frying pan and 'flavour' it with the remaining teaspoon of oil. Fry the fish in it for just a few seconds on each side; it should barely cook through. Arrange the beansprout mixture on the salad leaves and the slices of fish around this. Sprinkle with toasted sesame seeds and serve immediately.

Marinated kipper salad
SERVES 4

Use naturally smoked kippers which contain no added dyestuffs.

2 Manx kippers
1 lime
2 tablespoons olive oil

1 mild onion
Freshly ground black pepper
1 lb/450 g potatoes

Skin the kippers and remove the fillets as neatly as possible. Lay these in a shallow dish. Squeeze the lime and mix the juice with the olive oil (for which you could, of course, substitute walnut or hazelnut oil) and pour over the fillets. Peel and thinly slice the onion and lay on top of the fish. Grind on black pepper. The fish can now be left for some hours. Meanwhile boil the potatoes in their skins. When done and cool enough to handle, peel and slice. Divide among 4 serving plates and pile the marinated kipper and onions on top, with all the marinade.

Celeriac and mushroom salad with mussels
SERVES 4

24 large mussels
½ lb/225 g button mushrooms
1 lemon
½ lb/225 g celeriac
Lettuce and watercress
2 cloves garlic

3 tablespoons thick mild yoghurt
1 dessertspoon Dijon, tarragon or mild mustard
Salt, pepper
Fresh herbs as available

Scrub and rinse the mussels very thoroughly, knocking off any barnacles with the back of a knife blade. Tug off the beard. Put the mussels in a lidded saucepan over a high heat. Steam until open, about 2–3 minutes. Remove from the heat and strain off the cooking liquor to add to the salad dressing later. When cool enough to handle, remove the mussels from their shells and place in a bowl of cool water to stop them drying out.

Wipe the button mushrooms. If very fresh and white they should not require peeling. Slice or quarter them and sprinkle lemon juice over them. Peel the celeriac and cut into matchstick-size pieces or shred in the food processor. Drop into acidulated water immediately to stop it discolouring while you quickly prepare the rest of the salad.

Arrange watercress and lettuce on four plates. Crush the garlic cloves and add to the yoghurt. Beat in the mustard, salt and pepper. Drain the celeriac and stir into the dressing. Add the mushrooms.

You can, if you like, add a little of the mussel liquor for flavouring. Spoon the celeriac and mushroom salad over the lettuce. Drain the mussels and arrange these on top, garnishing with such fresh herbs as you have available. Serve immediately.

A brief, light olive oil and lemon juice marinade gives a surprisingly delicate quality to the smoked haddock. The same treatment can be given to kippers or other smoked fish. Apart from the basic salad leaves, the rest of the dish will depend on what you have available. When not much else is around I will add black olives, onion rings and capers. In season however, I have served quartered fresh figs with smoked monkfish. Smoked fish prepared in this way can also be served on squares of toast or pumpernickel as snacks to go with drinks.

Marinated smoked haddock salad
SERVES 4

8 oz/225 g smoked haddock fillet	1 small onion
1 tablespoon olive oil	Freshly ground black pepper
1 tablespoon (scant) lemon juice	Salad leaves
	Garnish to taste

Thinly slice the smoked haddock and lay the slices in a single layer on a plate or shallow dish. Sprinkle the oil and lemon juice over the fish, mixed together first if you wish but this is not important. Grind on a little black pepper. Peel and thinly slice the onion and lay the slices over the fish. Leave for at least 30 minutes, but not more than 1½ hours as the fish will become too impregnated with the marinade and so lose its translucence. Prepare four individual plates of salad leaves. Remove the fish from the marinade and carefully arrange it on the salad. Garnish as you wish, and pour on the marinade as a dressing, including the onion, separated into rings if you wish.

Halibut and spinach terrine
SERVES 6–8

8 large fresh spinach leaves	Seasoning
4 oz/100 g cooked drained spinach	Nutmeg
12 oz/350 g cooked halibut	2 oz/50 g cooked prawns, salmon, scallops, or anchovy fillets
½ pint/300 ml fish stock	
4 leaves of gelatine	

Blanch the spinach leaves very thoroughly to make them quite soft. Drain and dry them and use them to line a lightly oiled 1 lb/450 g loaf tin, leaving plenty of leaf to fold over the completed terrine. Soak the gelatine leaves in half the stock, and then melt it by heating gently. When completely melted, stir in the rest of the stock. Remove all skin and bone from the halibut and put it in the blender with two-thirds of the gelatined stock, a little seasoning and a pinch of fresh nutmeg. Blend until smooth and pour half the mixture into the terrine. Put to chill and set in the refrigerator.

Finely chop the spinach and mix with the rest of the gelatined stock. Dice the prawns, salmon or scallops and add to the spinach. When the terrine has set pour on the spinach and fish mixture. Let it set, then add the rest of the halibut mixture. Fold over the spinach leaves and return the terrine to the refrigerator until set. To serve, turn out on to a board or long dish and slice, serving 1 or 2 slices per person, with salad, mayonnaise or other sauce.

Salmon and watercress terrine
SERVES 8–12

1 lb/450 g whiting fillets, skinned	1 tablespoon chopped watercress
3 size-3 eggs	1 lb/450 g salmon fillets
10 oz/300 g *fromage blanc* or thick Greek yoghurt	2 oz/50 g cooked spinach – large leaves, kept as intact as possible
Seasoning	
2 oz/50 g shallots	5 oz/150 g blanched courgettes, cut into 1/4 in/ 1/2 cm strips lengthways
3 oz/70 g button mushrooms	
1 oz/25 g red pepper	

Process the whiting fillets until smooth. Add the eggs, *fromage blanc* or yoghurt and seasoning and process once more. Chop the shallots, mushrooms, red pepper and add, with the watercress, to the fish mixture. Process for 5–10 seconds.

Lightly salt and pepper the salmon fillets. Cut into 3 or 4 pieces that will easily fit the terrine. Wrap each piece in spinach leaves. Line the base of the terrine with some of the whiting mixture. Fill with alternate layers of courgettes, whiting mixture and spinach-wrapped salmon, leaving enough whiting for the top layer. Tap the terrine to allow the mixture to settle and bake in a *bain-marie* in a pre-heated oven, 150–170°C/300–325°F/gas mark 2–3, for an hour. Allow to cool and then refrigerate overnight. Serve in slices, with salad and perhaps some of the herb dip (see p. 41), or a similar sauce made with watercress alone.

1 medium sized sole, filleted
1 pint/600 ml fish stock
4 sheets gelatine or ⅔ oz/15 g
   powdered gelatine
2 firm tomatoes, skinned and
   de-seeded

1 medium red pepper, skinned,
   halved and de-seeded
4 oz/125 g very fine haricot
   beans
Fresh chives or watercress
2 tablespoons *crème fraîche* or
   soured cream

Terrine of sole
SERVES 4–6

When you buy the sole, have your fishmonger give you the bones and head, and a few extra bones to make a good rich fish *fumet* to which you could also, if you wished, add some white wine during cooking. This will make the jelly, so it needs to be clear and of a good golden colour, which I achieve by letting a piece of onion skin cook with the bones, but not for too long as it imparts a bitter flavour. Allow the stock to cool and then poach the sole fillets very gently for no more than 2 minutes. Cool in the stock until you can handle them. Remove carefully, drain on kitchen paper, trim the edges and divide each of the two fillets into four strips, lengthwise. Set aside. Strain the stock. To clarify it you can use the traditional method with egg whites, or use coffee filter papers.

In the stock, of which you will need 1 pint/600 ml, dissolve 4 leaves of gelatine (or ⅔ oz/15 g of powdered gelatine). Lightly oil a small loaf tin and pour in enough stock to generously cover the bottom of the tin. Allow to set.

While the first layer of jelly is setting, prepare the vegetables. Chop the tomato and pepper into neat dice and keep in separate piles. String and blanch the haricots. Unless they are very fine, split into two or three along the length. Wash and chop the chives if you have them, otherwise finely chop the watercress. The first layer of jelly should have set by now and you can begin to build up your terrine. For the next layer, pour on more stock and add the strips of beans so that they cover the whole surface. Allow to set (this can be done very quickly by placing in the ice-making compartment for a few minutes). The next layer should be half of the strips of sole and more stock; in the layer after that, use the tomatoes down one side, the peppers down the other, and chives or watercress in the middle. Once this has set, your last layer should be the rest of the sole with the last of the stock. Refrigerate until required.

To serve, unmould the terrine by gently shaking and tapping. It should slip out easily because you oiled it first. Slice and serve on individual plates, with one spoonful of *crème fraîche* to which you have added some chopped chives or watercress, and another to which you have added a spot of fresh tomato purée.

Mousse of Arbroath smokies
SERVES 6–8

The Arbroath smokie is a lightly smoked, undyed fish with a delicate flavour. It needs no further cooking.

2 smokies
¾ pint/400 ml fish stock
4 sheets of gelatine
6 oz/175 g sieved cottage
   cheese

2 egg whites
Seasoning to taste

Carefully remove all the flesh from the bones and put it in the food processor. Soak the gelatine in some of the stock and then melt it entirely. Add it and the rest of the stock to the fish. Process until smooth. Fold the sieved cottage cheese into the fish purée. Beat the egg whites to peaks and fold in gently. Taste and add salt or pepper.

Pour into an oiled fish mould if you have one, or into a loaf tin or a soufflé dish. Chill to allow it to set. When ready to serve, turn out on to the serving dish, perhaps on to a bed of shredded lettuce. Garnish with restraint.

Grilled skewers of fish with apple
SERVES 4 AS A STARTER, 2 AS A MAIN COURSE

A firm fleshed fish such as eel or monkfish is best. You can also add mushrooms, small tomatoes, prawns, or spring onions to the skewers, but I like the simple combination of fish and apple which works so well together, as in the salad on p. 74.

12 oz/350 g firm fleshed fish
   off the bone
2 crisp dessert apples
2 tablespoons apple juice

1 teaspoon sesame oil
Seasoning
1 tablespoon toasted sesame
   seeds

Cut the fish into bite-sized chunks. Core and quarter the apple and cut each quarter into two or three pieces, horizontally. Mix the apple juice and sesame oil together in a bowl. Add the fish and apple, coating it well with the marinade. Season lightly and let it stand in a cool place for half an hour or so. Thread the fish and apple alternately on small skewers and place under a moderate to hot grill for about 8 minutes, turning them and basting them occasionally with the marinade. When done arrange the skewers on one large dish or on individual serving plates, with a little salad perhaps, or if a main course with some fresh pasta or brown rice. Sprinkle with the toasted sesame seeds.

This is an expensive dinner party dish. I chose red mullet because the silvery pink underskin is kept on and looks lovely in the finished dish. Fillets of brill with a whiting *mousseline* and a flavoursome sauce would produce a less expensive version. It is the kind of dish which is open to many interpretations; sole or turbot with crab, lobster or langoustines, and the sauce could be a vegetable purée such as a red pepper sauce (see p. 55) or a simple reduction of fish stock. I have a weakness for this rather startling vanilla sauce, not sweet but sweet-smelling, which I have also served, together with a pistachio sauce, to accompany *boudins* of turkey.

Turban of red mullet with scallop mousseline and vanilla sauce
SERVES 4

1 pint/600 ml unsalted fish stock
1 vanilla pod
Fillets from a 1 lb/450 g red mullet, giving about 8 oz/ 225 g flesh
4 oz/120 g queen scallops or 4 scallops

2 shallots
Seasoning
2 tablespoons double cream
1 tablespoon unbeaten egg white
Melted butter
Chervil or other fresh herbs

Set the fish stock to simmer gently with the vanilla pod. Remove the outer skin from the two red mullet fillets. Cut each one into two lengthways and trim each piece to a neat strip, removing any bones. Clean the scallops and remove the white pad of muscle. If using queen scallops keep four to one side for garnish. If using the more common large scallops, chop half of one into fine dice to use for garnish. Put the rest of the scallops into a blender or food processor together with any trimmings from the red mullet (I usually find I have about 1 oz/25 g of trimmings left), the shallots, seasoning, one tablespoon of the cream and all the egg white. Blend until smooth and rub the mixture through a sieve into a basin. Check again for seasoning.

Brush four small moulds with melted butter. The size I use holds about 2½ fl oz/75 ml. Spoon a little of the scallop mixture into each mould, and then fit the half fillet of red mullet around the inside, filling the hollow with the rest of the *mousseline*. Tap smartly on the edge of the table to settle the mixture and put in a *bain-marie* in a moderate oven, 180°C/350°F/gas mark 4, for 15 minutes.

Finish the sauce at this point. Remove the vanilla pod from the stock and reduce this vigorously to about 2 fl oz/50 ml, or about 4 tablespoons. Cut the vanilla pod in half, and split one half down the middle. Scrape out the black seeds and add these to the sauce. Discard the empty half pod. Wash and dry the other half pod for future use. Put the scallops for garnish in a small strainer and steam them gently over the sauce to heat them through. Enrich the sauce with the rest of the double cream. This is, of course, optional. Divide the sauce between four medium-sized plates. Turn out the moulds, one on to each plate and garnish with scallops, plus a leaf or two of chervil or other fresh greenery.

Fish stew
SERVES 6–8

Use a mixture of shellfish and firm fleshed fish for this dish. Mussels, scallops, eel and monkfish are my preferred combination.

½ oz/15 g butter
3 good sized leeks
1 lb/450 g ripe tomatoes
3 shallots
4 cloves garlic (optional)
1 pint/600 ml fish stock
1 orange
½ teaspoon fennel seeds

about 1 quart/1 litre mussels
8 scallops
1½ lb/675 g eel
1½ lb/675 g monkfish
Seasoning
1 measure gin
Chopped parsley, chervil,
　chives or coriander

Melt the butter in a large, heavy pan. Thoroughly wash and trim the leeks. Cut them into shreds or rings. Peel, seed and roughly chop the tomatoes. Peel and chop the shallots, and garlic if using it. Put the vegetables in the pan and sweat them gently, moistening with stock from time to time, using up to half the stock in this way. Carefully remove the zest from the orange and cut it into long curving strips. Set this aside. Squeeze the orange juice and strain it over the vegetables and sprinkle on the fennel seeds. Put the lid on the vegetables while you prepare the fish.

Wash and scrub the mussels, tugging off the beard and knocking off any barnacles. Steam them in a lidded pan for 2 minutes until just beginning to open. Remove the pan from the heat and strain the mussel liquor over the vegetables. Remove the mussels from the shells and place them in a basin of cool water. Take the scallops from their shells and remove the pad of muscle and the intestine. Rinse quickly to get rid of any sand and pat dry.

Remove all skin and bone from the monkfish and eel and cut into bite-size chunks. Lay the chunks of eel and monkfish on the gently stewing vegetables, pour on the rest of the stock, seasoning and a measure of gin and continue simmering very gently for 10–15 minutes. Then add the scallops and cook for a further 3 minutes. Finally add the drained mussels and heat them through. Strew chopped herbs and the curls of orange peel over the fish and serve immediately.

Fish pie
SERVES 4–5

A dish which goes back to my very early cooking days, this is comforting to eat when you're cold, tired and hungry, particularly if you have to hand some freshly cooked spinach and freshly mashed potatoes. It is the kind of dish which I rarely make now, to the chagrin of one very dear friend who, I know, much prefers this sort of food to the rosy rack of lamb or tenderly pink *magret de canard* I am more likely to serve to him these days.

1½ lb/675 g smoked haddock fillet or finnan haddock
1½ lb/675 g potatoes

1 lb/450 g freshly cooked and drained spinach
½ oz/15 g butter
4 eggs
Seasoning

Poach the fish in milk or a mixture of milk and water, or steam it. When it is cool enough to handle, flake it and put to one side. Peel and boil the potatoes. Drain and mash until smooth. If you have poached the fish, add some of the poaching liquid to the potatoes to make them creamy. Make sure the spinach is fairly dry. Having

buttered an ovenproof dish, place the spinach in the bottom and lay
the fish on top. Separate the eggs. Beat the egg yolks into the potato
and season, perhaps also adding a grating of fresh nutmeg. Whisk
the egg whites until stiff and fold them gently into the mashed potato
mixture. Spread this evenly over the fish right to the edges of the
dish. Bake in the centre of a pre-heated oven for 15–20 minutes at
200°C/400°F/gas mark 5.

Lettuce wrapped mousselines of smoked haddock
SERVES 4

I use smoked fillets of haddock for this, but smoked cod could be
substituted.

4 large, firm lettuce leaves	2 tablespoons Greek yoghurt
7 oz/200 g smoked haddock	½ teaspoon cornflour
fillet	Ground pepper
1 size-3 egg	

Remove the hard stem from the lettuce. Blanch the leaves
thoroughly, drain and pat dry on kitchen paper. Lightly oil four
small ramekins or dariole moulds. Line each with a lettuce leaf,
leaving enough overlap to fold over the filling. Cut the fish into
chunks and put in the food processor with the egg and yoghurt
blended with the cornflour and ground pepper. Process until very
smooth and creamy. Ideally you should then push it all through a
sieve for a light fluffy texture to the *mousseline*. If you don't sieve,
you finish up with a firmer texture.

Divide the mixture amongst the four ramekins, fold the rest of the
lettuce leaves over the filling and place the pots in a roasting tin with
a little water in the bottom. Bake in the centre of a moderate oven,
180°C/350°F/gas mark 4, for about 20 minutes. When done, a knife
point inserted into the centre of the mould should come out clean.
Turn out on to individual plates, mopping up any liquid or draining
into whatever sauce you choose to accompany the mousselines. I
like to serve them with watercress or parsley sauce or a fresh tomato
coulis (see p. 54).

Shellfish in a paper bag
SERVES 4

Fish, and particularly something as delicate and fragrant as shellfish,
lends itself especially well to paper bag cookery. I love to cook
scallops with a little soy sauce, sherry, fresh ginger and spring onions
in a paper parcel for a fresh, oriental flavoured dish. Why not

combine whatever you have available to make an unusual first course? I would use partly opened mussels, some scallops, the biggest, juiciest prawns I could find, even a crayfish or langoustine each if possible. Use strong paper for these parcels.

½ oz/15 g butter
16 mussels in their shells
4 or 8 scallops, depending on
    size, or 16 queen scallops
8 prawns

4 crayfish or langoustines
4 tablespoons parsley
Seasoning
4 teaspoons white wine or
    lemon juice

Cut four 15 × 20 in/40 × 50 cm rectangles from baking parchment and fold each in half down the middle. Cut each piece of paper into a heart shape with the fold running down to the point. Melt the butter and brush over the paper hearts.

Scrub the mussels and knock off any barnacles. Put in a pan with a tightly fitting lid and steam over a high heat for a minute or two until they are just beginning to open. Remove from the pan and when cool place 4 on one side of each paper heart. Add the scallops, prawns and langoustines or crayfish. Sprinkle on the parsley and season lightly. Mix the wine or lemon juice with a little of the strained juice given off by the mussels. Sprinkle this over the shellfish.

The parcels are now ready to seal. Fold over the other side of the heart. With the edges together fold the paper over, making tight overlapping folds, or rolling the edges together to seal the parcel. Prepare the other parcels in the same way and lay them on a baking tray. Place it in a pre-heated oven, 200°C/400°F/gas mark 6, for 8 minutes. Serve while hot, placing each parcel on an individual plate and cutting them open at the table.

Scallops with julienne of vegetables
SERVES 4

1½ lb/675 g plump scallops
2 cloves garlic
1 in/2 cm chunk fresh ginger
1 carrot
1 leek

1 stick celery
Seasoning
½ lemon
2 tablespoons fish stock

Clean the scallops by rinsing thoroughly under cold water to wash away any sand. Remove the intestine and the thick muscle. Pat dry on kitchen paper. Place the scallops in a shallow pie dish. Peel and crush the garlic; peel and shred the ginger. Scatter over the scallops. Peel the carrot and trim the leek and celery. Cut each into very fine strips. Heap these on top of the scallops. Lightly season. Squeeze on just a few drops of lemon juice and moisten with the fish stock.

Place the pie dish on an upturned saucer in a frying or sauté pan. Pour in an inch of water or so. Cover with the lid or a sheet of foil. Bring to the boil and steam for 7–12 minutes, depending on how plump the scallops are and how well done you like them. Remove the scallops and vegetables and keep these warm on a serving plate. Slightly reduce the cooking juices and hand separately.

Steamed scallops
SERVES 4

This dish has a frankly oriental flavour, without being in the least authentic, since it mixes elements of Chinese and Japanese. A wok and steamer baskets would be the ideal equipment in that the whole thing could then be cooked on one burner, the scallops steaming over the vegetables steaming over the rice. You first start off with one tier as the rice takes longer to cook. Then halfway through, you add a basket of vegetables, then the scallops in a basket for the last few minutes.

The steaming medium is a mixture of soy sauce and rice vinegar added to water with some fresh ginger peelings and a couple of star anise pods. Use whichever rice you prefer – long grain, fluffy (basmati or Patna) or shorter grain, stickier rice. There's no reason why you shouldn't use brown rice either. The choice of vegetables is yours also. Prepare enough for four from the following: diagonally sliced carrots, broccoli florets, green beans, peas or mangetouts, long curls of carrot.

6 tablespoons rice vinegar	Piece of fresh ginger
4 tablespoons soy sauce	4 or 5 star anise pods
6 oz/175 g rice	4 spring onions
3 cloves garlic	8–12 scallops

Mix 2 tablespoons soy sauce and 3 tablespoons rice vinegar with 1 pint/600 ml water. Add 2 star anise pods and the ginger peelings and place in the pan or wok which is going to be the base of the steamer.

In another pan bring the rice to the boil in twice its volume of water and add half a teaspoon of salt. Simmer with the lid on for 10 minutes. Drain, rinse and drain again and place it in a steamer basket, lined with muslin if it has large holes. Steam the rice for 5 minutes and, while it is steaming, prepare the vegetables and place them in the second steamer basket which you fit on top of the rice. Steam the vegetables for 5–8 minutes while you prepare the scallops. Remove the pieces of tough muscle and any skin and dirt. Pat dry in paper towels. Put the scallops in the third steamer basket, and on top scatter the thinnest slivers of garlic and fresh ginger, with shreds of spring onions and 2 or 3 star anise pods. Sprinkle on a few drops of soy sauce. Place the third steamer basket over the vegetables, cover with a lid and steam for 3 minutes only. This is sufficient to cook the scallops. If you are using bamboo baskets, these can be brought to the table and everyone can help themselves using chopsticks and bowls. A dipping sauce can be made by adding a little chilli sauce to the remaining soy sauce and rice vinegar.

Cod fillets in orange and passion fruit sauce
SERVES 4

4 cod fillets, about 8 oz/200 g each, with the skin left on
1 orange
2–3 passion fruit
1 small onion or 2 shallots
Salt, pepper
4 tablespoons Greek yoghurt or *fromage blanc*

The unusual piquant flavour of the passion fruit blends well with that of the orange, and together they make an excellent marinade for the fish. Fillets of sea bass, sole or turbot prepared in this way would make a delicious fish for a dinner party. It is important that the fillets are roughly of the same shape, size and thickness.

Grate the zest from the orange on to a large shallow plate and squeeze on the orange juice. Cut the passion fruit in half and rub the contents through a sieve into the orange juice, reserving a dessertspoon of pulp and seeds for garnish. Peel and thinly slice the onion or shallot and place in a single layer on the plate. Place the cod fillets in the marinade, flesh side down, which you have just seasoned very lightly. Marinate for 30–40 minutes. Place the fish under a very hot grill, skin side up and grill for 8–10 minutes, depending on the thickness of the fillet and how well done you like fish.

Meanwhile, strain the marinade into a shallow pan and reduce until syrupy. Beat in the yoghurt or *fromage blanc*. When heated through, divide the sauce amongst four heated serving plates and lay a piece of fish alongside it. Garnish with herbs, capers, samphire or whatever you have available, with a little of the passion fruit pulp and seed. The anise flavour of fennel goes well with this dish; some fronds of fennel could garnish it, and a salad of fennel follows.

*Bacalhau
with olives,
garlic and
coriander*
SERVES 4

Some say that this is an acquired taste but it is one I seem to have been born with. I loved it the first time I tried it in Lisbon in 1972, and must have eaten it a dozen times during that visit; each time it was cooked a different way. A Portuguese friend, Eduardo, quotes his father's view that there are three ways of cooking *bacalhau*, 'há tres maneiras de cozinhar bacalhau: cozido, assado e estragado'. Boiled, baked, spoiled. Others will say that there are 365 methods of cooking dried salt cod, one for every day of the year. On the whole, I agree with Eduardo's father; the plainer the better. I did not much enjoy, for example, the creamy *bacalhau* with aubergines I tasted in one of Lisbon's better restaurants. And whilst *bacalhau con nata* is very popular, I enjoy it most of all simply baked in the oven with good olive oil, garlic and olives garnished with fresh coriander leaves and served with plain boiled potatoes. Just such a dish I had in Aviz on my last visit to Lisbon.

You can buy salt cod in Portuguese, Italian and Spanish shops. Buy more than you need and use the leftovers to mix with mashed potatoes, onions and coriander and make delicious fish cakes.

2 lb/about 900 g piece of salt cod	3 cloves garlic
	2 fl oz/50 ml olive oil
1 large mild onion	Fresh coriander leaves for
4 oz/100 g black olives	garnish

When you buy the salt cod, have them hack it into 4 or 5 pieces for you. It is extremely tough when dry, and difficult to cut unless you have extremely sharp knives and cleavers. Place it in a basin of water and soak overnight. Change the water from time to time.

Next day, drain the cod and trim off any fins and thin flaps. Shape into neat pieces and place in an earthenware dish or casserole. Peel and slice the onion and distribute the onion rings over the fish to cover it. Add the olives. Peel and crush the garlic and stir it into the olive oil. Sprinkle the oil over the fish and put it in a pre-heated oven, 180°C/350°F/gas mark 4, for 40–50 minutes until just tender. Timing will depend on the thickness of the fish.

Serve, garnished with fresh coriander, or parsley if this is not available, from the earthenware dish, accompanied by freshly boiled or steamed potatoes. New potatoes would go particularly well.

To my mind this rather dense textured, mild flavoured fish needs a piquant sauce, as well as careful cooking. A spoonful or two of the fragrant Chambéry vermouth adds a good herby flavour and the anchovies provide a welcome richness.

Halibut braised in vermouth and anchovy butter

SERVES 6

Cook enough fish to have leftovers to make a halibut and spinach terrine (see p. 77).

4 halibut cutlets each weighing 12–14 oz/350–400 g
1 onion
1 carrot
1 stick celery
1 pint/600 ml fish stock

1 oz/25 g butter
12 anchovy fillets
2 fl oz/50 ml Chambéry vermouth
Fresh herbs

Lay the four cutlets in a lightly oiled or buttered baking dish. Peel, trim and slice the onion, carrot and celery. Lay this on top of the fish and pour the stock over it. Place the dish in the top of a pre-heated oven, 180°C/350°F/gas mark 4, for 8 minutes.

Meanwhile soften the butter and pound the anchovies. Mix together. Remove the fish from the oven. Set aside 1 cutlet for use in a terrine. Remove the skin and central bone from the remaining three cutlets and arrange on another, smaller ovenproof dish. Keep warm while you reduce the cooking juices to about ¼ pint/150 ml. Add the vermouth and boil for a minute or two more. Spread the anchovy butter on the fish and pour the sauce over it. Return it to the oven and cook for 3–5 minutes more, depending on the thickness of the fish. Remove the dish from the oven, garnish with fresh herbs and serve immediately.

Cooking fish in a roasting bag removes the need even for the slightest trace of oil or butter and leaves you with no pots and pans to wash. I also like the very fresh tasting dishes produced by this method.

Mackerel with mustard and coriander

SERVES 4

4 mackerel, about 10 oz/275 g each
4 dessertspoons mustard
4 tablespoons finely chopped coriander or parsley or watercress

2 crushed cloves garlic – optional
Seasoning
4 dessertspoons wholemeal bread crumbs

The mackerel should be gutted and cleaned, heads on or off according to your preference. Slash each side diagonally in 3 places. Mix the mustard, coriander, garlic and seasoning and spoon it into the slashes. Press the bread crumbs into the surface. Use 2 roasting bags and place 2 fish in each, tightly closing the bag but cutting a slit in each to let the steam escape. Bake in a medium oven, 180°C/ 350°F/gas mark 4, for 25 minutes.

Mackerel fillets in a paper bag
SERVES 4

The ideal fish for this dish are ones that will give you small but thick fillets, weighing 6–8 oz/175–225 g each so that they do not overcook. Mackerel is robust in texture and flavour and can take other strong flavours, such as mustard, gooseberries, anchovies, all of which occur in mackerel recipes. I have used up ends of Parma ham with mackerel, added a few herbs and produced an unusual and tasty dish.

Olive oil   Seasoning
4 plump mackerel fillets   12 fresh sage leaves
2 oz/50 g thin slices of Parma
   ham

Cut four 15 × 20 in/40 × 50 cm rectangles from baking parchment and fold each in half down the middle. Cut each piece of paper into a heart shape with the fold running down to the point. Brush the oil over the paper hearts.

Trim the mackerel fillets to neat shapes, even if it means throwing some scraps away. Make three or four diagonal slashes in each fillet, on the skin side. Roll up small slices of Parma ham and stuff one into each slash. Lightly season the fillets, with very little salt if any, because the ham is already salty. Lay 3 sage leaves on each fillet, between the slashes, and place each one on one side of each paper heart.

The parcels are now ready to seal. Fold over the other side of the heart. With the edges together fold the paper over, making tight overlapping folds, or rolling the edges together to seal the parcel. Prepare the other parcels in the same way and lay them on a baking tray. Place it in a pre-heated oven, 200°C/400°F/gas mark 6, for 10 minutes. Serve while hot, placing each parcel on an individual plate and cutting it open at the table.

In this dish the tartness of the rhubarb fulfils the same sort of need for the tastebuds as lemon in other fish dishes. Buy from the 'shoulder' end of the fish to give you a thick, even chunk.

Noisettes of monkfish with rhubarb
SERVES 4

1½–2 lb/675–900 g monkfish	¼ pint/150 ml fish stock
½ oz/15 g unsalted butter	Seasoning
2 or 3 sticks rhubarb	1 tablespoon finely chopped parsley

Skin the monkfish very thoroughly, removing all gristle and gelatinous skin. Cut from the central bone, leaving you with two thick fillets. Cut each into 4 equal slices. Gently heat the butter in a frying pan. Peel the rhubarb and cut into slender batons about 2½ in/ 7 cm long and cook gently in the butter for 2 or 3 minutes. Remove and keep warm. Place the slices of monkfish in the pan in a single layer and cook gently for 6–8 minutes, turning once. Remove with a slotted spoon while you quickly finish off the sauce.

Add the fish stock to the frying pan which will also contain some cooking juices from the monkfish. Reduce by half over a high heat. Season to taste. Strain on to heated dinner plates, arrange the monkfish and rhubarb on top and garnish liberally with chopped parsley, which is important for the overall flavour of the dish.

Cooked in the oven like a leg of lamb this produces a succulent alternative to the traditional roast. And by enclosing the fish in a roasting bag you ensure that all the cooking juices, flavour and moistness are retained.

Roast monkfish with anchovy stuffing
SERVES 4

1 lemon	1 oz/25 g black olives
1 tablespoon olive oil	2 oz/ 50 g peeled, seeded, chopped tomatoes
1 monkfish tail weighing about 2 lb/900 g	Garlic and seasoning to taste
4 oz/100 g ricotta	Pinch of thyme, oregano or marjoram
1 oz/25 g chopped anchovies	

Remove all the skin and gristle from the fish. Mix the juice of the lemon and the oil and marinate the fish in this for an hour. Carefully loosen the bone without separating the fish entirely into two. Keep the bone in place.

Mix the ricotta with the anchovies. Stone and chop the olives and mix this into the ricotta, with the tomatoes, garlic, seasoning and herbs. Stuff the fish with this mixture and tie it together at six or eight places down the length. Put the fish inside a roasting bag, close it and place it in a roasting tin in a pre-heated oven, 170°C/325°F/ gas mark 3. Cook for 50 minutes. Remove from the oven and keep in a warm place for 5 minutes to relax it. Cut the string and remove the bone which should now slide out quite easily. Slice into rounds and serve immediately.

Medallions of monkfish in parsley sauce
SERVES 4

Buy the thick end of the fish so that you can cut neat, regular slices.

1¾ lb/800 g monkfish
Pinch of curry powder
Good handful of parsley

5 fl oz/150 ml rich fish stock
Seasoning

Remove all the skin and underskin from the monkfish if this hasn't already been done. It is important to do this, otherwise it will shrink and toughen during cooking. Remove the central bone which will give you two fillets of fish. Cut each into 4 or 6 rounds. Pat them dry and season with a little curry powder.

Cook the fillets gently in a non-stick frying pan, or with a little butter in an ordinary frying pan if you prefer. When cooked, remove from the pan and keep them warm, covered to stop them drying out. Strip the parsley from the stalks, chop it roughly and add to the pan, together with the stock. Cook for just a minute or two to tenderise the parsley. Put it with the liquid into a blender and blend until smooth. Sieve or not, according to your taste and divide amongst four heated serving plates. Serve 2 or 3 fillets of monkfish on the sauce.

A purée of sorrel or fresh tomato make good alternatives to the parsley.

Salmon steaks with red wine and tarragon sauce
SERVES 2

Certain fish take kindly to a red wine, both in the sauce and to drink with it. Salmon is one of them. For the sauce I would use the same wine as I was serving with the meal, either a classic Bordeaux or a Chinon. The latter is excellent for cooking as it does not change its colour quite as much as other red wines do. It is the wine I use for *coq au vin* and other winy dishes. Extravagant? Not too extravagant, since I rarely cook with wine now. When it is an important part of the dish, as in this recipe, then I like to use a good one.

If you use a non-stick frying pan this will reduce the amount of butter required to about ½ oz/15 g, just enough to give the sauce a little body and unctuousness.

2 salmon cutlets, weighing 6 oz/175 g each	Tarragon leaves for garnish
¼ pint/150 ml good red wine	Seasoning
1 tablespoon chopped tarragon	½ oz/15 g unsalted butter

Heat a frying pan and, when quite hot, lay the salmon pieces in it. Turn the heat down and cook the fish very gently for 3–4 minutes. Raise the heat again and carefully turn the salmon. Cook on the other side for 2–3 minutes, first on a high heat very briefly, then with the heat turned right down. Cooking time will depend on the thickness of the cutlets and how well done you like your fish. Remove the fish from the pan, leaving the cooking juices behind, and keep it in a warm place while you finish the sauce by turning up the heat, adding the wine and deglazing the pan with the help of a spatula or wooden spoon. Let the wine reduce by half. Add the tarragon, season to taste. Away from the heat, add the butter bit by bit, stirring vigorously until the sauce thickens slightly. Divide it between two heated dinner plates. Place the salmon on top and garnish with the rest of the tarragon leaves.

Lemon poached salmon trout
SERVES 6–8

A fish kettle or deep roasting pan are the best containers in which to poach fish. This recipe is the one I use when I want to serve a cold fish with salad. The poaching liquid makes an excellent base for a fish soup to which you can add any left-over salmon trout. The flavouring comes not from lemon juice, but the essential oils and fragrance from lemongrass, if you can find it in oriental greengrocers or supermarkets, or lemon balm and lemon verbena.

3 lb/1.4 kg salmon trout	Thinly pared zest of a lemon
2 or 3 pieces lemongrass or 3 good sprigs lemon balm or lemon verbena	Salt and peppercorns

Have the salmon trout cleaned and gutted. Wipe it thoroughly inside. Place the lemon grass and lemon balm or verbena on the rack in the fish kettle. Tuck the lemon zest inside the fish and lay it on top of the rack. Cover with cold water. Add a little coarse sea salt and a few peppercorns. Parsley stalks and a couple of bay leaves can be added too. Bring the water slowly to the boil, let it bubble two or three times only, then remove from the heat and allow the salmon trout to cool in the stock. When cold, remove carefully on to a serving plate, skin and garnish. Reserve the cooking liquid for use in a soup, see p. 28.

Sea bass
with samphire
SERVES 4

Until recently, if you wanted samphire you had to go to Norfolk and the other places where it grows wild, and for free, by the sea-shore. Now, if you are prepared to pay the high prices, you can buy it in London. I am told by the fishmongers who sell it that it is the suppliers who set the high prices, not the fishmongers. Samphire is so delicious that I usually serve it by itself, mounds of it, simply steamed and served with melted butter. As an extra special treat, I serve it with a sea bass. Cooking the two together produces a wonderful exchange of flavours.

Ask your fishmonger to clean and scale the fish. The head should be left on. For this recipe you really need a fish kettle, but could improvise with a grill pan, rack and foil.

2 lb/900 g samphire
2½ lb/1.2 kg sea bass
White pepper

Wash the samphire thoroughly in several changes of water. Cut off the root system. Fill the fish kettle to just below the rack. Cover the rack with the samphire. Place the fish on top and sprinkle lightly with pepper. Place some of the samphire on top of the fish. Cover with the lid. Bring the water to the boil and steam the fish gently for 30–35 minutes.

When cooked, carefully lift the fish on to an oval plate, and surround it with samphire. Show it to your guests in its natural state and then remove it, and yourself, to the kitchen. Fillet the fish and serve on individual plates on a bed of samphire, with melted butter if you wish. You can also serve it cool with good mayonnaise.

Rich in iodine and smelling of the sea, laver bread is one of those things like samphire that, once tasted, immediately became one of my favourites and something to be sought out from fishmongers or sent for from Wales. It is now available in tins and also fresh in Selfridges. As a sea vegetable it has an affinity with fish and I have experimented with it in a number of ways, making sauces for white fish, stuffing mussels with it, mixing it into pasta dough to serve with shellfish. It is delicious mixed, in a small quantity, with pounded anchovies, butter and garlic and spread on hot toast as an appetiser.

Here is a treat for the single diner. Quantities can, of course, be increased to stuff more sole. And you will know what size of sole you can eat. The bacon is optional, as is the butter.

Sole with laver bread
SERVES 1

1 Dover sole
1 tablespoon laver bread
1 tablespoon brown
  breadcrumbs

1 rasher smoked bacon, finely
  chopped
Plenty of ground pepper but
  no salt
½ oz/15 g unsalted butter

Gut and skin the sole but leave its head on. With a sharp knife slit down on either side of the backbone and ease the flesh away from each side of the bone for about ½ in/2 cm. Mix the rest of the ingredients and stuff this between the bone and the flesh. Slip the fish inside a roasting bag and place in a pre-heated oven, 180°C/350°F/gas mark 4, for 10–15 minutes depending on the thickness of the fish. Serve, with the cooking juices poured over it, accompanied by boiled, steamed or baked potatoes.

In this dish the steam is scented with an infusion of herbs or a *tisane*, one of the herbal teas now widely available here, either loose or in sachets. My own favourite is a mixture of lemon verbena, mallow flowers, rose buds and orange flowers.

Fillets of sole in lettuce with saffron sauce
SERVES 4
AS A STARTER,
2 AS A MAIN
COURSE

Other fish can be substituted for the sole; small turbot, witch sole, lemon sole, brill etc. Have the fish filleted and keep the head and bones for stock, together with any other bits that your fishmonger will give you.

1 medium to large Dover sole
Seasoning
4 ripe tomatoes
2 shallots or 4 spring onions
8–12 large lettuce leaves

1 tablespoon dried or fresh
  herbs or *tisane* mixture
5 fl oz/150 ml fish stock
Pinch of saffron stamens

Make a stock from the sole bones. Skin the sole fillets if your fishmonger has not done this and add the skin to the stock pot. Cut each fillet in half lengthways, and dry thoroughly on kitchen paper. Season very lightly. Peel and de-seed the tomatoes. Chop into quite small dice. Finely chop the shallots or spring onions and mix with the tomatoes. Put to one side in a sieve over a bowl, to let any excess liquid drain off.

Prepare the lettuce leaves by cutting out the base of any firm central rib which would make it difficult to roll the leaf. Place all the leaves in a colander and blanch them by gently pouring boiling water over them. This is much easier than trying to do it in a pan. Drain the leaves and when they are cool enough to handle, spread out two or three at a time, overlapping them. Take one fillet of sole and, on its widest end, place a tablespoon of the tomato mixture. Roll the fillet carefully around the mixture and place it on the lettuce. Fold the lettuce leaves around the fish to make a neat parcel, completely enclosing it. Do the same with the other 3 fillets.

Place the parcels in a steamer basket. Bring a pan of water to the boil, throw in the *tisane* and place the basket in the pan so that it is above the water level. Cover tightly and steam for 5–8 minutes.

Meanwhile, make a light sauce by steeping the saffron in a little fish stock. Add any tomato liquid to the rest of the fish stock and reduce this until almost syrupy. Add the saffron liquor, season to taste, bring back to the boil and serve a little surrounding each parcel of sole. Garnish with a few strips of carrot which you could steam on top of the fish.

1 sole, weighing a good 1 lb/ about 500 g
2 shallots or 1 small onion
6 oz/175 g button mushrooms
1 clove garlic
1 tablespoon finely chopped parsley
Seasoning
A little freshly grated nutmeg
5 oz/150 ml strong fish stock

Fillets of sole with mushroom stuffing
SERVES 2

Fillet the sole or have your fishmonger do it for you. Season lightly and set aside in a cool place. With a chopper or in a food processor chop the mushrooms, shallots (or onion) and garlic until very fine without making a purée of them. Cook the vegetables, moistened with a little stock if necessary to stop them sticking, preferably in a non-stick frying pan. When cooked, allow to cool slightly. Stir in the parsley and season to taste.

Lightly oil an ovenproof dish, or two individual dishes. Take each of the four skinned fillets in turn, smooth side up. Place a quarter of the mushroom mixture on half the fillet and fold over the other half. Place carefuly in the dish. Continue with the other 3 fillets. Cover the dish or dishes with foil and bake in a pre-heated oven, 220°C/425°F/ gas mark 7, for 8–10 minutes. Meanwhile reduce the stock until syrupy and no more than 2 tablespoons. Season to taste. Remove the fish from the oven, carefully draining any cooking juices into the reduced stock, and not letting the mushroom filling escape. Reduce the sauce again if necessary. Strain it over each of the fish fillets, grate a little fresh nutmeg on top and pop under a very hot grill, just long enough for the glaze to brown a little.

Game, poultry and other meat

'Pork. Water. Rusk. Egg. Salt. Starch. Sugar. Sodium Phosphate E450(a). Spices. Preservative E223. Flavour enhancer – Monosodium glutamate. Antioxidant E300. Herb extracts. Colour E120' ran the list of ingredients attached to the 'prize winning recipe' pork sausage I had for breakfast some months ago. Cleverly packaged to look like a bag of the home-made sausages you might bring home from your favourite country butcher, I was completely taken in by them. They tasted salty and artificial and I could not eat them. A far cry from good honest butcher's meat, which is what I shall stick to when I want to treat myself to meat. And yes, I do still like meat. Occasionally. In small quantities.

I look for game, poultry and lean meat. Meats from naturally-reared animals, free-range poultry and game answer, in part, my qualms about eating meat at all. To my mind these are the tastiest meats as well as being more nutritionally sound. Some of them are much underrated. Rabbit, pigeon and hare can be cooked in many ways, to produce elegant dishes for dinner parties, or simple straightforward dishes for a family supper, such as the game casserole on page 108. The pigeon with sweet and sour vegetables (p. 104) is striking in its unusual flavours and its appearance, yet quite inexpensive.

Lamb is not a particularly lean meat, but I do find the loin of lamb one of the easiest to trim of all fat, and it has a most delectable flavour which I much prefer to even the grandest fillet steak.

Poultry now is much improved in flavour. Not long ago the only tasty chickens to be found were those maize-fed birds, imported from France. It is now possible to find good free-range local chickens and turkeys, so all those favourite recipes which were long since put to one side can be brought out again and new ones developed. Cooking poussins in coarse salt is an old, old method, a good one which retains all the flavour and the juices (see p. 110). But you must have a good chicken to start with. (Incidentally, whole fish can be cooked very successfully in the same way.) The finished dish is not salty, as the salt crust comes right away from the meat.

I had not cooked turkey for many years until I was commissioned to write a piece about using turkey in ways different from the traditional Christmas roast. I have included some of my recipes here because, once you forget about turkey as a monolithic whole, it becomes a collection of various cuts of meat, low in fat, versatile, nutritious and, with imagination, the basis of tasty dishes.

It is important to cook good basic ingredients simply so that they taste of themselves and are not hidden by a sauce, or overcooked, or swimming in butter or oil. I generally grill small cuts of meat or 'fry' them, with little or no oil in either an old, heavy, black frying pan that is well-seasoned after years of use, or a non-stick frying pan. Clear roasting bags are also very useful and clay pots can be too. Although here I must sound a note of caution: in my experience the instructions given for these clay cooking pots require one to cook things for far too long and at too high a heat. I find that not only are they uneconomical but also tend to overcook things, if the instructions are followed. I usually cook with them in a considerably lower oven.

This is a wonderful combination of wild autumn flavours, a fleeting treat to be seized in September and early October. Too early in September and the duck will not have had time to hang; too late in October and the blackberries will be woody and 'have the Devil in them'. And there is the debate about whether to cook the breasts on or off the bone. Some argue that, in doing the latter, you lose some of the flavour. I think if I had the oven on anyway, I would roast the bird whole; if not, I would either remove the breasts and cook them in a non-stick frying pan, or spatchcock the bird and grill it. Whichever way I did it, I would use the rest of the bird, that is, the meat on the legs, for a game sauce, and the carcass for stock.

Wild duck breasts with blackberry sauce
SERVES 2

Another way would be to grill the spatchcocked bird, remove the breasts and serve those with their appropriate accompaniments, and grill the legs a little longer, serving them on a bed of salad.

6 oz/175 g large ripe blackberries	1 wild duck
2 tablespoons wine vinegar	¼ pint/150 ml stock
2 tablespoons red or white wine	Seasoning

Pick out 2 oz/50 g of the best blackberries for garnish. Place the rest in a basin and pour over the wine vinegar and the wine. Crush the berries and leave them to stand overnight. Next day rub them through a sieve. Brush some of the resulting purée on the duck breasts and roast or grill the bird in whichever way you have decided.

When done to your liking, keep the breast warm and make the sauce. Reduce the stock to about 2 tablespoons, stir in the rest of the blackberry purée, heat through and pour on to hot serving plates. Arrange the sliced duck breast on top and garnish with the whole blackberries.

Roast saddle of hare with apples
SERVES 2–4 (DEPENDING ON SIZE)

You can occasionally find frozen saddles of hare, but far better to buy the whole thing and have your butcher joint it, leaving the saddle whole. With the rest – fore-legs, hind legs and giblets – you have plenty of ingredients for excellent game soup, pâté or a sauce for pasta (see p. 30).

1 saddle of hare	1 tablespoon juniper berries
10 oz/300 ml apple juice	Chives or other herbs
1 sliced onion	

Marinate the saddle overnight in the juice together with the onion, juniper berries and herbs. Remove the hare from the marinade which you strain and set aside for the sauce. The final cooking takes very little time so have everything else ready that you might be serving with the hare. Heat the oven to 230°C/450°F/gas mark 8. With a sharp knife ease the fillets gently away from the chine bone, without removing them. This makes carving easier. Put the hare, in a roasting tin, into the hot oven and roast for 15 minutes. Remove from the oven and let it rest in a warm place while you prepare the plates. Slice the hare into thin diagonal slivers and serve with the following sauce.

The sauce

1 onion	1 dessert apple, peeled and
A little olive oil	sliced
Liver from the hare	The marinade
2 oz/50 g chestnut purée	Seasoning

Slice and fry the onion until browning nicely. Add the apple slices. Chop the liver and add it, together with the chestnut purée. Cook together to make a rich 'stew', adding the marinade and letting it reduce considerably. Season to taste and serve with the hare.

As a pasta fan I would almost certainly use any left-over hare to make a rich, gamy sauce, to serve with pappardelle, the broad, flat home-made pasta. Pheasant, pigeon and wild duck can be used in exactly the same way.

Hare sauce for pasta

8 oz/225 g hare off the bone	1 oz/25 g raisins – optional
1 tablespoon olive oil	1 dessertspoon pine nuts or
1 sliced onion	almonds – optional
2 cloves garlic	Sprig or two of fresh
5 fl oz/150 ml red wine,	marjoram or pinch of dried
marinade, stock or gravy	oregano
1 small square bitter dessert	
chocolate	

Cut up the hare into small thin strips. Heat the oil and fry the sliced onion until browning. Stir in the hare and brown it all over on quite a high heat. Chop the garlic or crush it in salt and add it together with the wine or stock. Bring to the boil and then turn the heat down very low, allowing the mixture to simmer very gently. Add the chocolate and let it melt into the sauce which will not taste chocolaty as a result, but will take on a certain richness. Pine nuts and raisins add interesting flavours and textures if you want to use them. Finally add the oregano and cook the sauce for at least 40 minutes. The meat will be tender and falling into shreds. Taste for seasoning, and serve with your favourite pasta.

Stuffed breast
of pheasant
SERVES 4

2 hen pheasants
12–16 large lettuce leaves

Stuffing

4 dessertspoons cooked brown
rice
4 dessertspoons chopped,
peeled, de-seeded tomatoes
2 dessertspoons soft
wholemeal breadcrumbs
2 dessertspoons grated apple
Pinch of marjoram, oregano or
thyme
Salt and pepper to taste

Infusion

Handful of fresh herbs or
1 dessertspoon mixed dried
herbs
Zest of an orange, thinly
peeled

Carefully remove the breasts from the pheasants and skin them. (For what to do with the rest of the pheasant, see p. 99). Slit each breast almost in half and open it out butterfly fashion. Press it flat. Using a non-stick or well-seasoned cast-iron frying pan, seal the meat, cooking it on a high heat for 30 seconds on each side. Blanch the lettuce leaves by arranging them carefully in a colander and pouring boiling water over them to make them soft and pliable for wrapping. Trim out the base of the hard central rib. Pat the leaves dry on kitchen towels.

Mix all the stuffing ingredients together and divide among the four pieces of meat. Fold together and re-form into the neat pouch-shape it was before you slit it and secure with half cocktail sticks. Wrap each breast completely in three or four lettuce leaves and place in a single layer in a steamer basket. Set this over a pan of water containing the herbs and orange peel, cover tightly with the lid or foil and steam gently for 20–25 minutes.

Serve each parcel, sliced if you wish, on a heated dinner plate, with a little fresh pasta and a spoonful of tart fruit jelly such as apple or quince, or some home-made apple purée. A few spoonfuls of reduced stock made from the pheasant carcass after you've removed the breast and legs makes the best possible gravy.

For this cooked marinade, I would use the wine I was serving with the meal, possibly a Loire wine from Chinon or Bourgueil, or a Rhône, a Crozes-Hermitage or a Saint-Joseph. Côte Rôtie would be just a little too good for the marinade. With practically as much meat on them as partridge or grouse and at a tiny fraction of the cost, pigeon is not only very good value but delicious, and it surprises me that it is not served more often.

Pigeon breasts in red wine
SERVES 4

4 pigeons
2 tablespoons olive oil
1 onion
1 carrot
1 stick of celery
Piece of fennel bulb – optional
Parsley stalks
2 or 3 cloves of garlic
Pinch of cumin seeds –
    optional

Sea salt
Black peppercorns
5 fl oz/150 ml red wine
½ square of dark chocolate
1 tablespoon fruit jelly, quince,
    gooseberry, crab apple etc.
6 tablespoons stock
½ oz/15 g butter – optional

Gently heat the olive oil in a saucepan. Slice, dice or roughly chop the vegetables, including the garlic and parsley stalks, and add to the olive oil. Cook until the onions are just beginning to turn light brown. Add the salt, pepper and cumin, if you are using it. Pour in the wine and bring to the boil, allowing it to reduce very slightly. Remove from the heat and leave to cool. While the marinade is cooling prepare the pigeons. Remove the breasts carefully from each bird, dry and place in a bowl. Brown the carcasses in a heavy pan, add water and make up a good, strong stock. You will only need a little for the sauce, but the rest will keep, say, for a game soup another day. When the marinade is relatively cool to the touch, pour it over the pigeon breasts and stand the dish in the fridge or a cool place overnight.

The final cooking does not take long at all, so have everything else to hand, and the rest of your meal practically ready. Remove the pigeon breasts from the marinade and dry thoroughly on kitchen towels. Strain the marinade and put to one side to use for the sauce. I would add the vegetables (which will also be well marinaded) to the stock you are already preparing.

Heat a non-stick frying pan. When hot place the pigeon breasts in it, skin side down, in one layer. Reduce the heat after a minute and cook for 2 to 3 minutes more. Raise the heat and turn the breasts over. Cook until you judge them done to your liking. There is nothing wrong in serving pigeon slightly rosy. Remove the meat from the pan and keep warm on a plate. Keeping the frying pan on a high heat, add the strained marinade, the chocolate, the fruit jelly and the stock. Stir together and boil fiercely to reduce to a syrupy sauce, which you can, if you like, finish off by adding tiny pieces of butter and swirling it around the pan.

To serve, spoon a little sauce on to each heated dinner plate. Slice each pigeon breast in half horizontally, arrange four pieces on each plate, with a spoonful of the jelly used in the sauce, and your chosen accompaniments.

A variation on this theme can be used for chicken breasts. Use white wine for the marinade and add a few chopped olives to it. Before cooking the chicken you can slit each breast to make a pocket, and fill with a little of your favourite stuffing.

Pigeon breasts with sweet and sour vegetables
SERVES 4

4 plump, tender pigeons	2 leeks
6 or 8 crushed juniper berries	4 oz/100 g mushrooms
Ground black pepper	1 dessertspoon soy sauce
2 celery hearts or 6 sticks celery	1 dessertspoon brown sugar
8 oz/225 g white cabbage	1 dessertspoon rice vinegar (or sherry vinegar or wine vinegar)
2 carrots	

Carefully remove the breasts from the pigeons. Season with freshly ground black pepper and the crushed juniper berries. Peel and finely slice or shred the vegetables. Place in a steamer basket, with the mushrooms on top and steam until tender but not soggy.

Meanwhile cook the pigeon breasts, either in a non-stick frying pan, a well-seasoned cast-iron pan or under a hot grill for 3–4 minutes on each side. Allow to rest in a warm place on a plate. When the vegetables are cooked, tip them into a bowl. Mix together the soy sauce, sugar and vinegar and stir this into the vegetables until they are well coated and the sugar has melted. Divide between four heated dinner plates. Slice each breast in two, and arrange four slices on each plate, pouring over any cooking juices which have collected on the plate.

Use the pigeon carcasses to make a rich tasty stock.

Buy two rabbits if you want to serve 4 as a main course. Have the butcher leave the saddle whole. Use the legs for pâté or in a casserole.

Roast saddle of rabbit with herbs and ricotta

SERVES 2 AS A MAIN COURSE OR 4 AS A FIRST COURSE.

1 rabbit
Seasoning
Bunch or packet of prepared
  watercress

3 oz/75 g ricotta cheese
1 teaspoon Dijon or other
  good, strong mustard
1 clove garlic

Bone the saddle by cutting with a sharp knife on each side of the backbone and scraping along and down over the ribs, easing the flesh off the bones. When you have finished you should have two long fillets of lean meat, each with a thin flap. Season the meat lightly and lay one piece next to the other, flaps overlapping. Wash and dry the watercress. Remove any damaged or yellowing leaves and the coarsest stalks. Finely chop and mix with the ricotta cheese and mustard. Add a crushed garlic clove. Spoon the mixture on to the flap and spread evenly. Slip 4 or 5 lengths of twine under the meat, bring the two edges together and tie together as a roll in 4 or 5 places, making sure that the filling is not oozing out of the ends. Slip the meat inside a roasting bag which you have slit in one or two places. Secure it tightly and place on a baking sheet in a pre-heated oven, 180°C/350°F/gas mark 4, and roast for 25 minutes.

Remove from the oven and allow to rest in a warm place for 10 minutes before slicing into neat rounds and serving with any cooking juices and some vegetables. I like to serve something green and crisp, like squeaky beans or crunchy broccoli, and something soft like a parsnip and potato purée.

If you make the stuffed saddle of rabbit above and have bought a whole rabbit, you will be left with ribs, shoulders and hind legs. With these make a delicious cold terrine of rabbit, excellent for a buffet luncheon, or indeed as a starter at any kind of meal. The best I've ever tasted was at La Charmille in Châtellerault where Madame Proust presides over a small, beautifully run restaurant whilst her husband, Christian Proust, consistently turns out some of the most delicious food I've ever eaten. His set menu gives just enough choice for two people to sample eight different dishes.

Jellied rabbit and vegetable terrine

SERVES 8

1 lb/450 g rabbit meat off the bone

1 pint/600 ml seasoned chicken, vegetable or rabbit stock

3 oz/75 g fine green beans

3 oz/75 g carrots

3 oz/75 g celery

3 oz/75 g peeled, seeded tomatoes

4 sheets leaf gelatine or 4 level teaspoons powdered gelatine

Trim the rabbit and cut it into long strips. Put three quarters of the stock in a saucepan and gently poach the rabbit for 5 minutes, allowing it to cool in the liquid. Top and tail the beans. Peel the carrots and cut into long, thin strips and then into matchsticks. Remove the stringy bits from the celery and cut into strips. Remove the rabbit from the liquid and poach the vegetables in the stock for 3 minutes, until tender. In the rest of the stock soak the gelatine until soft. When softened, stir it in to the still warm stock in which the vegetables have been poached, and from which they have been removed. Melt the gelatine thoroughly.

All is now ready for assembly. Take a 1½–2 lb/650–900 g loaf tin and oil it lightly. Pour a little gelatine into the bottom of the tin and lay in enough beans to cover. Allow to set. Lay the carrots and celery strips on top and pour in some more stock. When this has set, add the rest of the rabbit and some more stock. When set, add the final layer, which is stock, and the diced tomato. Allow to set in the refrigerator. To serve, turn out the terrine and serve a slice per person, perhaps with a herb sauce, an uncooked tomato *coulis* or watercress sauce (see p. 54).

Rabbit sauce for pasta
SERVES 4–6

Having bought a large rabbit to prepare the boned, stuffed saddle on p. 105, you may not feel like preparing the jellied rabbit terrine (p. 105). Here is a tasty sauce for pasta using the rest of the rabbit, the hind- and forequarters. The carcass goes into the stock pot.

Rabbit liver, heart and kidneys

1 lb/450 g rabbit off the bone

1 medium sized onion or 2 or 3 shallots

3 oz/75 g mushrooms

2 ripe tomatoes or 4 tablespoons fresh tomato *coulis*

Seasoning

¼ pint/150 ml good stock

Trim the giblets and soak them in a small bowl of milk for 30 minutes. Trim any fat and sinews from the rabbit pieces and slice thinly. Peel and slice or finely chop the onion or shallots and sweat in a non-stick frying pan. When translucent, add the morsels of rabbit. Cook on a fairly high heat to brown them and then turn down the heat. Remove the giblets from the milk. Dry and slice them and add to the frying pan. Cook gently for 2–3 minutes and then add the sliced mushrooms. If using fresh tomatoes, pour boiling water over them to remove the skins then rub them through a sieve into the meat sauce. Or add the tomato *coulis*. Add the stock a little at a time, whilst cooking the sauce for a further 15–20 minutes on a low heat. Season to taste, perhaps adding a few fresh herbs, finely chopped.

Rabbit with lavender
SERVES 4

Michel Guérard steams rabbit over an infusion of hyssop. Rosemary or sage or other strongly scented herbs would also make an appropriate infusion, but if you can get hold of fresh lavender, I think you will enjoy the results. Use the saddle and hindquarters only, cut into four joints. My husband Tom suggests cooking frog's legs by this same method.

20 sprigs of fresh lavender
  flowers
1 pint/600 ml water

1 young rabbit
Seasoning

Bring the water to the boil and drop in three quarters of the lavender flowers. Bring back to the boil, then remove from the heat. Allow to infuse for 20 minutes. Place the cleaned, trimmed and lightly seasoned rabbit in a steamer basket and place this over the lavender infusion. Cover the whole pot with a tight fitting lid. Bring the liquid to the boil and then simmer gently allowing the rabbit to steam for some 25 minutes. A wild rabbit may take a little longer than a tame one. Keep it warm while you prepare your chosen accompaniments. I would serve it with a little compote of fresh wild mushrooms which would make their own sauce, or perhaps a mixture of dried wild mushrooms and button mushrooms, with a few lightly steamed haricot verts, a spoonful of home-made rhubarb and lavender jelly and perhaps a little brown rice, or better still wild rice. Garnish with the rest of the lavender flowers.

Noisettes of venison with passion fruit

SERVES 4

The loin of venison, from which the *noisettes* are cut, is meat of such good quality, texture and flavour that it needs only the lightest marinade, if any. This marinade is based on fresh passion fruit juice which gives the finished sauce a light fruity flavour. I have used the same method for preparing *aiguillettes* of wild duck.

4 slices of loin of venison, about 2 in/5 cms thick, weighing 5–6 oz/150–175 g each

4 passion fruit
Nutmeg
¼ pt/150 ml stock
Seasoning to taste

Cut the passion fruit in half. Squeeze the halves on a lemon squeezer to extract most of the juice. Rubbing the seeds in a sieve will extract a little more. Grind a little fresh nutmeg over each piece of venison, place in a dish and pour the passion fruit juice over it. Stand in a cool place for a couple of hours. Remove from the marinade and dry each piece. Heat a non-stick frying pan, and when hot, put in the venison. Cook on a high heat on both sides until it reaches the stage of doneness you require. Remove and keep warm. Pour the stock into the hot pan and reduce by half. Add the marinade, season and reduce further to taste. You can slice the venison or serve it whole, surrounded by a little light sauce. Serve with suitable accompaniments. Shredded celeriac cooked almost to a purée is particularly good with venison; a crisp vegetable would go well, and one of your favourite clear fruit jellies.

Game casserole

SERVES 4–5

Instead of hare, a mixture of hare, pheasant, venison and wild rabbit can be used. Walnuts make a good substitute for the pine nuts.

1½ lb/675 g hare
1 dessertspoon olive oil
2 onions

½ pint/300 ml game stock
1 oz/25 g raisins
1 oz/25 g pine nuts

Trim the meat of any sinews and gristle and cut into even-sized pieces. Fry it very quickly in the olive oil until sealed all over. Put it in a heavy ovenproof casserole. Fry the onions until browning, and pour on the stock. Bubble until this is slightly reduced, scraping up any bits stuck to the pan. Add the raisins and nuts and pour over the meat. Cook in a low oven, 170°C/325°F/gas mark 3, for 40–50 minutes.

Braised red cabbage is delicious with game, so too is sliced Jerusalem artichoke braised in a little stock. Serve a crisp salad, perhaps fennel and orange, to start with.

If fresh dill is not available, you could use dried dill weed or dill seeds and change the title of the recipe.

Breasts of chicken with dill and lemon gin sauce

SERVES 6

2 lemons with good skins	5 oz/150 ml chicken stock
2 oz/50 ml gin	Bunch of dill
6 chicken breasts, removed from whole chickens	2 tablespoons *fromage blanc*
½ oz/15 g unsalted butter (or a non-stick frying pan)	

Heat the gin to just below boiling point. Grate the lemons into it and allow to infuse for a few hours or overnight.

Remove the skin from the chicken breasts and trim off any sinews, fat and gristle. Heat the butter in the frying pan or, preferably, heat a non-stick frying pan. Place the chicken breasts in a single layer and cook on one side, on moderate heat, for 5–8 minutes. Turn over and do the same on the other side. The cooking time will depend on the thickness of the meat. Provided it is done over a moderate heat, the dish will not suffer from being left to cook a little longer. Remove the chicken breasts when done, and keep hot. Add the strained lemon gin and the stock to the frying pan, chop up the dill (but keep a few sprigs for garnish) and add it. Reduce the sauce until quite syrupy in texture and with a good flavour. Enrich with the beaten *fromage blanc* if you wish; this will give a pale, creamy, opaque sauce, rather than a translucent one.

You can serve the chicken breasts sliced diagonally and fanned out on each plate, but it is also quite nice to serve a 'cushion' of chicken garnished with the fronds of dill, sitting in a pool of sauce.

Strong dry vintage cider which we'd bought on a drive through Herefordshire and which, on tasting, we found rather too powerful for us, was the inspiration for this recipe. It also coincided with a glut of quinces, not the large knobbly pear-shaped fruit but the small fragrant yellow Japonica quinces given to me by a friend. After I'd made 16 jars of clear amber jelly, some with and some without

Chicken with cider and quinces

SERVES 4–6

rosemary, I started to think of other ways of using them up. A couple
tucked inside a chicken being braised in vintage cider is one way.
Flavoursome apples or pears could substitute for the quince.

3 lb/1.35 k. fresh, free-range
   chicken
3 cloves garlic – optional
½ lemon

Salt, pepper, paprika
½ pint/300 ml strong dry cider
2 small quinces

Trim the chicken of excess fat. Cut off the tips of the wing pinions,
any loose skin and do whatever else needs to be done to make your
chicken presentable for the table. Peel and slice the garlic, if you are
using it, and cut each slice into thin slivers. Insert them under the
skin at intervals. Rub the half lemon all over the chicken, squeezing
out the juice on to it. Sprinkle with salt sparingly, more liberally with
pepper and paprika. Put the cider in a small saucepan and reduce by
half, thus getting rid of the alcohol and concentrating the flavour.
Heat a non-stick frying pan and in it seal the chicken all over. Put the
halved fruit inside the chicken, put the chicken in a lidded casserole
and pour the cider over it. Cover and cook the chicken in a pre-
heated oven, 200°C/400°F/gas mark 6, for about an hour. When
cooked, remove the chicken from the casserole and keep it warm on
a carving plate. Reduce the cooking juices until syrupy and serve
these separately in a heated sauceboat.

If liked, you could cook some carrot sticks along with the chicken
for the last half hour and serve them as one of the vegetables.

*Poussins
baked in salt
with whole
garlic cloves*
SERVES 2

2 x 12 oz/350 g poussins
8 large, unpeeled garlic cloves

3 lb/1.5 kg coarse salt – i.e. in
   crystals

Wipe and trim the poussins. Untruss them, as I find this allows them
to cook through more evenly. Trim the garlic cloves of their outer
skin but do not peel right down to the flesh.

Line a roasting tin with foil. I have a tin about 8 x 12 in/20 x
30 cm which is a perfect size for two poussins. Spread half the salt in
the bottom of the tray and make two poussin-sized indentations in
it. Lay the birds in these and press well down. Tuck the garlic cloves
into the salt too. Cover the poussins and garlic with the rest of the
salt, packing it well down to form a crust. Bake in the centre of a pre-

heated oven at 200°C/400°F/gas mark 6 for 45 minutes.

Lift the foil out of the roasting tin and place on a serving dish, folding the foil back under the salt crust. Crack open the salt when you are ready to serve and lift the poussins out on to heated dinner plates. The skins will be crisp and brown, and all the juice inside. The salt comes away as a crust. The garlic cloves will be soft and melting in their skins and not at all pungent. With this I serve *small* baked potatoes (small so that they will cook in the 45 minutes that the poussins are in the oven). Split the potatoes in half and spread with soft garlic instead of butter. A revelation.

Stuffed squabs SERVES 2

This is a rather expensive bird but is delicious, quick to cook and the carcasses make excellent stock afterwards. You could substitute the smallest 12 oz/350 g poussins and allow a slightly longer cooking time. What you stuff them with depends on what you have available; anything from an exotic stuffing of cooked wild rice and wild mushrooms to fresh brown breadcrumbs with lots of herbs and garlic. Quails or partridges can be prepared in the same way.

2 squabs
1 onion
3 oz/75 g brown bread
1 tablespoon sieved cottage cheese
2 tablespoons chopped fresh herbs
Seasoning
2 tablespoons stock or water

Cut the wing tips from the birds and wipe them thoroughly, inside and out. Peel and finely chop the onion. Mix this with the brown bread, cottage cheese, herbs and seasoning. Stuff into the cavity of the birds and secure the flaps closed with cocktail sticks. Heat a non-stick frying pan and brown the birds all over. Transfer them to a casserole. Deglaze the pan with stock or water, scraping up any residue. Pour it over the birds, cover the casserole and cook in a moderate oven 190°C/375°F/gas mark 4 for 35 minutes. New potatoes can be baked at the same time and make a perfect accompaniment.

Boned and stuffed turkey thighs
SERVES 2

Thighs from a 5 lb/2.25 kg turkey will serve 2.

2 turkey thighs
½ mango
2 oz/50 g celeriac or celery,
   blanched and cut into strips
Parsley
1 tablespoon brown
   breadcrumbs

Salt, pepper
½ pint/300 ml turkey stock
Pinch saffron
Julienne of leeks
Purée of sweet potatoes,
   carrots and cardamom

Cut a slit down the length of the thigh and carefully remove the bone, scraping all the flesh away. Open out the resulting square and flatten it with a rolling pin. Remove as many sinews as possible. Prepare the other piece in the same way. Peel the mango and cut into long strips. Lay the mango and celeriac down the middle of the boned thigh. Mix the parsley, breadcrumbs and seasoning with enough stock to moisten. Divide between the two boned thighs and press it down over the mango and celeriac. Roll up each piece of meat and tie round in four places with kitchen string. Place the two rolls in a roasting bag, seal and place in a pre-heated oven, 190°C/ 375°F/gas mark 5 for 35 minutes.

Remove carefully from the roasting bag, pouring the cooking juices into the turkey stock. Keep the meat warm while you finish the sauce. Reduce the stock by half and strain on to the saffron in a small clean saucepan. Reduce further until syrupy. Remove the string from the rolls and slice each into 5 or 6 rounds. Arrange on heated dinner plates, with a *julienne* of leeks, the sauce and a little purée of sweet potato, carrot and cardamom.

Turkey and sweetbread terrine with tomato and ginger coulis
SERVES 4–8

Makes a 1 lb/450 g terrine.

4 oz/100 g lamb's sweetbreads
10 oz/275 g turkey breast
   meat
2 'fillets' removed from the
   turkey breast
Turkey liver and heart
2 tablespoons *crème fraîche* or
   double cream

1 egg
Salt, pepper, nutmeg
1 heaped tablespoon finely
   chopped coriander or
   parsley
Fresh tomato *coulis* (see p. 54)
2 pieces crystallised ginger

Soak the sweetbreads for 30 minutes or so in water to which you have added the merest pinch of salt. Rinse. Put in a pan of cold water and bring slowly to the boil. Simmer for 30 seconds, remove from the heat and plunge them into cold water. Drain and press between two plates.

Prepare the rest of the meat by trimming all the sinews from the breast and the fillets, and any fat or gristle from the giblets. Cut the heart and liver into strips, and set aside, together with the fillets. Trim the sweetbreads by removing sinews and pieces of fat, cutting off any small pieces to leave neat oblong nuggets. Chop the breast meat into 1 in/2 cm chunks and put in the food processor with the cream, seasoning and egg. Process until smooth.

Lightly oil a 1 lb/450 g loaf tin and put in a third of the turkey mixture. Lay the turkey fillets on top towards the middle and cover with a little more of the *farce*. Press in strips of turkey liver and heart, down the length of the terrine. Spread more *farce* over it, leaving one-third. Roll the sweetbreads in the chopped coriander and make sure that they are completely covered with the herb. Lay the pieces of sweetbread on the terrine leaving about $\frac{1}{4}$ in/$\frac{1}{2}$ cm all the way round. Cover completely with the rest of the turkey *farce*. Tap well down. Set in a roasting tin containing a little water and place in a pre-heated oven, 150–170°C/300–325°F/gas mark 2–3 for 1 hour. Remove, then allow to cool. Refrigerate until required, making sure that you allow it to come back to room temperature in time for serving. Few dishes are less appetising than cold slabs of terrine straight from the fridge.

To serve, unmould on to a board and cut one slice per person. Serve on medium-sized plates, not huge deserted dinner plates, surrounded by a little sauce. This is an extremely delicately flavoured terrine and I would not want to serve too assertive a sauce with it. I like to accompany it with an unusual tomato *coulis*. I take a small piece of crystallised ginger, chop it finely and add it to the lightly cooked tomatoes which I then blend and sieve. As a garnish, I thinly slice and then cut into fine strips another piece of crystallised ginger, and serve a little pile of this with each slice of terrine.

Turkey breast with scallops and coral sauce

SERVES 4

2 breasts from a 5 lb/2.25 kg turkey
10 oz/275 g scallops
2 tablespoons thick yoghurt
1 tablespoon chopped chives
2 tablespoons chopped, peeled and de-seeded tomatoes

1 dessertspoon egg white
½ pint/300 ml turkey stock
10 oz/275 g broccoli florets, lightly steamed
Fruit jelly, such as lavender and rhubarb, or quince and apple

Carefully remove the breasts from the carcass without tearing the meat, as you want to use the piece of meat as a pocket to be filled. Slits and holes are no good, as the stuffing will burst out when cooked. From each breast take the club-shaped fillet which you can save for another dish, such as the turkey and sweetbread terrine. At the oblique, narrower edge of the breast make a deep slit, opening up the whole of the breast inside without piercing the edges.

Remove the coral from the scallops and set aside. Remove the small chunk of muscle from each scallop as well as any other inedible bits. Chop the scallops into small cubes. Mix with half of the yoghurt, the chives, tomatoes and lightly whisked egg white. Spoon the filling into the turkey breasts and close the opening with cocktail sticks. Flatten the breasts slightly.

In a non-stick frying pan cook the stuffed breasts for 30 minutes, turning several times to allow each side to brown gently. You can moisten with a little stock from time to time. When done, remove the breasts and keep them warm while you finish off the sauce. Add the rest of the stock to the cooking juices in the pan and gently poach the scallop corals for 1 minute. Remove and put them in the blender with the rest of the yoghurt and a tablespoon of stock. Blend until smooth, sieve and set aside. Reduce the contents of the frying pan over a high heat until you have about 3 tablespoons syrupy sauce. Remove it from the heat and pour it into a small basin over a pan of hot water. Whisk in the coral sauce and keep it hot without allowing it to boil.

Have four heated dinner plates ready. Slice the turkey breasts across into neat diagonal slices. Spoon some sauce on to each plate. Arrange a few slices of turkey breast on each plate and garnish with lightly steamed broccoli florets. A little jelly can be handed separately.

This is a very simple dish which, if prepared at home in the morning, would be ideal to eat in the garden at lunchtime or take on a picnic. Lovage has an assertive celery flavour. It combines particularly well with ham and new potatoes. Two steamer baskets, one on top of the other, are used here.

Ham with lovage
SERVES 4

Good handful of lovage leaves (or celery tops)

1 joint of ham or smoked pork weighing 1 lb/450 g off the bone

New potatoes – allow 6 small ones per person

Celery hearts – 1 per person

Fresh peas – optional

Fresh parsley for garnish

Soak the ham for 2–3 hours or overnight, to get rid of excess salt. Rinse. Place in a steamer basket in a pan of water containing the lovage leaves. Cover with a lid, bring to the boil, and lower the heat and keep the water at a very gentle simmer. The ham should cook slowly for 25 minutes per pound, plus an extra 25 minutes. Fast cooking will shrink the tissue and make the meat tough. About 15–20 minutes before it is ready, place another steamer basket on top containing the scrubbed new potatoes and trimmed celery hearts. Cook until tender, perhaps adding a few handfuls of fresh peas just before the end. Allow to cool in the baskets, and serve cold with other picnic food. This is also delicious hot.

For this slow cooking casserole, use boned shoulder of lamb trimmed of as much fat as possible. Served with steamed bulgur wheat and a crisp salad, this is a well-balanced main course containing plenty of fibre.

Spiced lamb and flageolet casserole
SERVES 4

8 oz/225 g dried flageolet beans

1 lb/450 g lean lamb

1 tablespoon olive oil

1 onion

2 cloves garlic

½ teaspoon cumin seeds

½ teaspoon coriander seeds

½ pint/300 ml stock

8 dried apricots

Seasoning

Parsley or coriander

Soak the beans overnight. Next day drain them and put into fresh cold water. Bring them *very* slowly to the boil, over a period of about 45 minutes. This is a good method of tenderising them.

Meanwhile prepare the casserole. Cut the trimmed lamb into 1 in/

2 cm chunks. Heat the olive oil to smoking point (or use a non-stick frying pan) and sear the meat on all sides. Remove it to an ovenproof casserole. Fry the sliced onion and chopped garlic without browning either. Add the spices and cook these for a few minutes. Pour in the stock and let it reduce slightly. Cut the apricots in two and add to the stock. Season lightly with salt and pepper and pour over the meat. Add a tablespoon of chopped parsley or, better still, coriander. When the beans have come to the boil drain them and add them to the lamb. Bring the whole casserole to the boil and then put it in a low oven for 2 hours at 170°C/325°F/gas mark 3. You may need to top up with a little more stock or water. Serve sprinkled with some more fresh herbs.

Lamb and pomegranates
SERVES 4

8 *noisettes* of lamb – about 1 lb/450 g total weight, cut from the loin, trimmed of all fat and gristle
2 or 3 pomegranates (depending on size)

1 onion, peeled and thinly sliced
Black peppercorns
Pink peppercorns – optional
Garlic – optional and to taste
4 tablespoons rich meat stock

Place the *noisettes* of lamb in a single layer in a shallow dish. Cut the pomegranates in half. Pick the seeds out of one half and keep these intact for decoration (about 1 dessertspoonful per plate). Squeeze the rest on a lemon squeezer and strain the juice over the lamb. Add the onions, crushed peppercorns and garlic to the marinade. Stand for a few hours or overnight.

Remove the lamb from the marinade which you strain into a small saucepan. Heat up the grill and cook the lamb under quite fierce heat, turning it over once, so that it is quite brown, but not burnt, on the outside, and moist and pink inside. Keep the meat warm while you finish off the sauce by adding the meat stock to the marinade and bubbling it hard until syrupy. Divide the sauce amongst four heated serving plates, place the lamb on top, scatter a few pomegranate seeds over it and serve immediately.

Lamb tagine
SERVES 4

This dish, essentially a casserole, can be prepared the day before, and gently reheated. Coriander is a vital ingredient if you want a truly authentic flavour for this north African dish. If you cannot buy *harissa*, a hot purée of peppers usually sold in small tins or tubes, mix 1 tablespoon of paprika with half a teaspoon of cayenne pepper, and moisten with a little oil to make a paste.

1½ lb/675 g boned shoulder of lamb	2 cloves garlic
2 tablespoons seasoned flour	2 teaspoons *harissa*
2 onions	¾ pint/400 ml of stock
2 carrots	Salt and pepper to taste
1 stick celery	Coriander leaves and/or ½ teaspoon seeds
2 tablespoons olive oil	½ teaspoon cumin seeds

Cut the meat into neat chunks. Heat the oil in a heavy casserole. Shake the meat in a paper bag with the seasoned flour. When the oil is hot, put in the meat and sear all over at a high temperature. Remove the meat and do the same thing with the chopped or sliced vegetables. Add half the stock, lower the heat and stir, scraping up all the residue from the pan. Return the meat to the vegetables in the pan, add either the paprika and cayenne mixture or the two teaspoons of *harissa*, then the rest of the stock. Add the coriander leaves or crush the coriander seeds and add these – about a teaspoon will do – along with the cumin seeds.

Cook in a medium low oven 170°C/325°F/gas mark 3 for 1½ hours. When ready to serve, season to taste. Serve in a shallow bowl and garnish with coriander leaves. Plain, boiled potatoes accompany this rich stew very well. Warm pitta bread can also be served, as can any other good, fresh bread.

Iscas
SERVES 4

This recipe for cooking liver is from Lisbon and is one of my favourite ways of preparing it. Rather than calves' liver (which does not lend itself well to a marinade) I use best quality lamb's liver. The secret is to cook it very quickly so that it does not toughen. It is delicious served with steamed, boiled or baked rice.

1½ lb/675 g lamb's liver	2 fl oz/50 ml olive oil
2 fl oz/50 ml white wine or 1 tablespoon wine vinegar	1 mild onion
	Seasoning

Remove any piping from the liver and cut first into slices and then into strips about the size and thickness of your little finger. Place in a basin. Stir the wine or wine vinegar with the olive oil and pour this over. Peel and thinly slice the onion and add to the liver. Leave to marinate overnight.

Take a heavy casserole with a lid, and preferably with handles, and heat this on the stove. Drain the liver, reserving the marinade. Put the liver in the hot casserole, perhaps doing it in two or three batches so as not to crowd the pan which would lower the temperature and the meat would steam instead of searing. Put the lid on and shake the casserole vigorously. Return it to the heat to cook for no more than 3–4 minutes. Remove the liver and keep warm. Proceed in the same way until you have cooked all the meat. When you have removed the last of the liver from the casserole, pour in the marinade, boil until reduced by half and pour this over the liver. Serve immediately after lightly seasoning.

Pork and bean
casserole
SERVES 4

Pork is at its most tasty and succulent when cooked in a low oven and slowly, and so is ideal for clay pot cookery. Beans have always been a classical accompaniment. Fresh orange juice, orange peel and coriander are added for flavour.

$\frac{3}{4}$ lb/350 g soaked cannellini
   beans
4 spare rib chops, about
   $\frac{1}{2}$ lb/225 g each
1 onion
1 stick celery

2 oranges
1 teaspoon coriander seeds
$\frac{1}{4}$ pt/150 ml stock
Seasoning
1 tablespoon fresh coriander
   leaves

Soak the clay pot for 15 minutes in cold water. Place the soaked beans in the base. Using a non-stick frying pan, brown the spare rib chops all over, if necessary first trimming off any surplus fat. Lay them on top of the beans. Peel and slice the onion and celery and brown them lightly in the frying pan. Add to the pork and the beans. Remove several strips of zest from one of the oranges and bury these among the beans. Cut the oranges in half, squeeze the juice and strain it into the casserole. Crush the coriander seeds and sprinkle on top. Add the stock. Cover the casserole and cook in a pre-heated oven 170°C/325°F/gas mark 3 for 2 hours. When cooked, season to taste and serve garnished with plenty of chopped coriander.

This is a lighter and more luxurious version of an old favourite. The oysters are added for fun and in memory of those times when everyone could afford to eat oysters, so abundant were they. I have used fresh, tinned and even smoked oysters, each giving a different sort of flavour and texture.

Steak, kidney and oyster pudding

SERVES 4 or 5

For the pastry
4 oz/125 g stone ground, self-raising flour
4 oz/125 g wholemeal breadcrumbs
Pinch of salt
2 oz/50 g frozen margarine or butter
¼ pint/150 ml cold water

For the filling
1 lb/450 g rump steak
½ lb/225 g veal kidney
1 onion
¼ lb/125 g button mushrooms
¼ pint/150 ml stock
Seasoning
Pinch of thyme
6 oysters

Sift the flour into a bowl with the salt and stir in the breadcrumbs. Grate or chop the margarine or butter and stir it into the dry mixture. Using a knife stir in enough water to make a light dough. Turn it out on to a lightly floured board and knead it gently before gathering it together into a ball. Leave, covered, while you prepare the meat.

Trim the steak and kidney and cut into 1 in/2 cm chunks. Thinly slice the onion and sweat in a non-stick frying pan until soft and just turning colour. Turn up the heat and add the meat, turning to seal it on all sides. Add the mushrooms, stock, seasoning and herbs. Let it simmer together for 5 minutes, then remove from the heat and allow to cool. Roll out the pastry, keeping some of it for the lid, into a circle about ¼ in/½ cm thick and with a slightly wider diameter than that of the basin. Lightly oil a 2 pint/1 litre pudding basin and line it with the pastry. Spoon in the cooled filling and arrange the six oysters on top. Roll out a pastry lid, cover and pinch the edges together. Cut out a circle of greaseproof paper to well cover the basin. Pleat it in the middle and secure with string. Put the basin in a large saucepan or steamer and pour in boiling water half way up the basin. Steam, gently, with a lid on for 1½ hours. Just before the end, place a steamer basket of greens on top and cook for 8–10 minutes. Serve with the pudding.

Sweet treats

I feel it is right to call this selection of pudding recipes treats. Treats are something to be looked forward to on special occasions, not something to be expected every day. Few people have the time to make a pudding for every dinner or lunchtime. Indeed, few people really want to eat a delicious, home-made sweet everyday. Fresh fruit finishes most of our meals at home, or perhaps nuts and dried fruit in the wintertime.

These simple ingredients can be dressed up to make fruit salads or compotes. This is when dried fruit comes into its own. Lovely compotes in autumn colours, rich in flavour and full of good healthy fibre. The drying concentrates the natural fruit sugars so no extra sweetening is needed in these dishes. I particularly like to make up unusual combinations, perhaps sticking to one colour as in a soft fruit salad with strawberries, raspberries and redcurrants, or a golden salad of orange, papaya and mango. Different varieties of single fruits are effective too, such as a mixture of different melons, especially if you can find bright ruby watermelon to include with the pale green honeydew and the creamy, peach colour of the canteloupe.

Making more elaborate use of the fresh ingredients, you can turn them into fruit pies. Combine them with creams or yoghurts to make light fools. Fruit purées can be used as the basis for a mousse, or even a hot soufflé instead of the flour-based *panada*. They can be made into sorbets or served as an accompaniment to light, airy *coeurs à la crème*. Some fruits are extremely high in fibre, for example mangoes, papayas, apricots and raspberries.

Cream can be replaced with yoghurt, sieved cottage cheese, *quark*, smatana which are delicious in their own right. Some manufacturers are now producing low-fat cream substitutes, with half the calories of the cream, but which seem to have the texture and close to the flavour of cream. However, I do find I have a built-in prejudice to a manufactured 'natural' product and so, if the flavour and texture of cream is essential to a dish, I will use the real thing. In the same way that there is no substitute for chocolate. These are after all treats so, just occasionally, I might serve just one white chocolate truffle after dinner.

It was, I think, my mother's scepticism about the possibilities of making a decent sponge with wholemeal flour which led me to persevere with adapting my standard fatless sponge recipe. Instead of white flour I now use a mixture of wholemeal flour and, in the recipe given here, ground hazelnuts and a little baking powder. Four whole eggs are replaced by 2 whole eggs and 3 egg whites and I use only a quarter of the amount of sugar normally used in the sponge.

Natural fruit juices can be used in place of sugar syrups and honey, particularly if you reduce them slightly to concentrate the flavour. Wonderful fruit jellies can be made in a loaf tin rather than the traditional jelly mould, and a slice served on an individual serving plate with a garnish of fresh fruit, mint or a fruit sauce.

With a little care and imagination, it is possible to finish a meal on a high note with a delicious and wonderful-looking pudding without piling on too many calories.

Prepare the syrup the day before required.

Apple and melon in ginger honey
SERVES 4–6

1 small chunk fresh ginger	3 crisp, red dessert apples
2 tablespoons clear honey	½ lemon
2 tablespoons water	1 small, ripe melon

Peel and slice the ginger, then cut into tiny strips. Heat the honey and water to boiling point. Add the ginger and simmer it for 2 minutes. Remove from the heat and allow to macerate overnight.

Next day quarter and core the apples and slice them into a glass bowl. Sprinkle with lemon juice. Cut the melon in half, remove the seeds and scoop out balls or cut into chunks. Add to the apples and pour on the syrup. Chill for an hour or two before serving.

Apple and mincemeat pancakes
SERVES 6

Another way of using up Christmas mincemeat.

For the batter	For the filling
2 oz/50 g self-raising flour	6 dessert apples
2 oz/50 g wholemeal self-raising flour	Cinnamon
1 egg	Nutmeg
½ pint/300 ml skimmed milk	2 tablespoons honey
2 oz/50 g mincemeat	

Beat the flour, egg and milk together to make a smooth batter. Stir in the mincemeat and let it stand for 30 minutes or so. Meanwhile prepare the filling. Here I use dessert apples, but you can vary this according to what you have available – pears and walnuts, stewed apricots, even ice cream.

Peel, core and slice the apples, not too thinly. Dust with cinnamon and nutmeg and cook them gently in a non-stick frying pan. When almost done add the honey and let this melt over the apples.

Make the pancakes in the usual way, fill with a spoonful of the apple mixture, fold over and serve immediately.

Baked apricots with vanilla
SERVES 4

It is difficult to buy perfect fresh apricots in England. Usually they come to us a little under-ripe and lacking that warm, musky flavour. Cooking them helps, particularly this way, in paper parcels in the oven. I generally cook them with a vanilla pod and a hint of lime, lemon or orange juice. You could put on a dab of honey, a spoonful of rum, orange liqueur, almond liqueur or whatever pleases you.

½ oz/15 g butter	1 vanilla pod
12 apricots	1 orange

Cut four 15 × 20 in/40 × 50 cm rectangles from baking parchment and fold each in half down the middle. Cut each piece of paper into a heart shape with the fold running down to the point. Melt the butter and brush this over the papers. Cut the apricots in half and twist the stone out. Pile 6 apricot halves on to one side of each paper heart. If you have the energy, crack open the stones and extract the kernel. This will give a wonderful flavour and scent to the finished dish. Cut the vanilla pod into 4 and lay one piece across each pile of apricots. Grate the orange zest on top, then cut the orange in half and squeeze the juice over the apricots.

The parcels are now ready to seal. Fold over the other side of the heart. With the edges together fold the paper over, making tight overlapping folds, or rolling the edges together to seal the parcel. Prepare the other parcels in the same way and lay them on a baking tray. Place it in a pre-heated oven, 200°C/400°F/gas mark 6, for 10 minutes. Serve while hot, placing each parcel on an individual plate and cutting it open at the table.

Cranberry, pear and walnut pudding
SERVES 6–8

Early in November the first of the cranberries begin to be imported from America. At the same time our own walnuts and pears are at their best. Here is a recipe for combining them in a pleasing way.

8 oz/225 g fresh cranberries
2 ripe pears
4 oz/100 g walnut halves
3 oz/75 g unrefined granulated sugar

3 large eggs
4 oz/100 g sifted wholemeal, self-raising flour
2 oz/50 g melted unsalted butter

Wash and pick over the cranberries. Drain and pile on a clean tea-towel to dry. Peel, core and slice the pears. Mix them with the cranberries, walnuts and 1 oz/25 g of sugar and put them in a buttered baking dish, about 2 in/4 cm deep and about 2 pints/1.15 l capacity. Beat together the eggs, the rest of the sugar, the flour and butter until smooth and pour over the fruit. Bake for 45–50 minutes in a pre-heated oven at 170°C/325°F/gas mark 3 until risen and golden. When done, a knife-point inserted into the centre will come out clean.

Cranberry sorbet
SERVES 4–6

This is a tangy, unusual sorbet which is good at the end of a rich meal. Made with less sugar, it could well be served between courses. Red or black currants, raspberries, bilberries and strawberries can be treated in the same way.

1 lb/450 g fresh or frozen cranberries	4 oz/100 g honey, warmed
	1 lemon

Wash the cranberries and put in a heavy pan. Just cover with water. Simmer the fruit until soft. Then add the warmed honey. Stir until melted. Add the juice of a whole lemon. Make a purée of the fruit in a blender and rub it through a sieve. Cool completely. When cool freeze in a *sorbetière* or icecream maker according to instructions, or pour into a plastic, lidded box and freeze. During freezing, beat it from time to time to stop ice crystals from forming.

Green fruit salad

This is simply a mixture of all the good green fruit you can find available:

Muscat grapes	Star fruit
Sultana grapes	Passion fruit seeds
Green apples	Melons
Green pears	

Served in a glass bowl with twists of lime, passion fruit seeds and, for the syrup, simply a few spoonfuls of good fruit juice – apple or pear perhaps, as these are nice and clear.

Mango mousse
SERVES 4–6

If the mango is very ripe the dish should be sweet enough without adding any sugar.

1 pint/600 ml clear apple juice	2 egg whites
4 leaves gelatine	Sugar to taste
8 oz/225 g cottage cheese	Toasted, flaked almonds
1 ripe, fragrant mango	

First soften the gelatine in a little of the apple juice. Then heat ¼ pint/ 150 ml of apple juice and add the softened gelatine and juice, stirring until dissolved. Sieve the cottage cheese and put it in the blender. Peel the mango, catching as much of the juice as possible in the blender, to which add the fruit pulp, the gelatine mixture and the rest of the juice. Blend until smooth. Whisk the egg whites until stiff and fold into the mango mixture. Add sugar to taste. Pour into a dish, chill and set. Garnish with toasted almonds.

4 leaves gelatine
1 pint/600 ml unsweetened
  grape juice, bottled or from
  a carton

4 scented geranium leaves –
  optional
½ lb/225 g large muscat grapes

First soften the gelatine in a little grape juice. Then heat ¼ pint/150 ml of juice and stir in the softened gelatine and juice until melted. Pour, with the rest of the juice, into a jug or basin and allow to cool. Spoon a shallow layer into the bottom of a wetted 1 lb/450 g loaf tin. When almost set, lay in the washed and dried leaves, veined side uppermost. Allow to set. Peel the grapes and remove the seeds. Cut most in half but leave some whole. Place a layer of grapes on the set jelly and pour on some more liquid. Allow to set. Then add another layer of grapes and liquid, continuing until all the fruit and liquid are used up. Chill until set. To serve, turn out on to a long dish, garnish as you will and slice on to individual serving plates.

The flavour of these little, wrinkled brown shells is so intense and piercing that a little goes a long way.

6 passion fruit
1 teaspoon cornflour
Up to 2 oz/50 g caster sugar,
  to taste

3 size-3 eggs and 2 extra egg
  whites
A little butter

Cut the fruit in half and rub the pulp through a sieve over a bowl to obtain the juice. I quite like to stir a few of the crunchy seeds into the soufflé mix, but you may prefer not to, in which case discard the seeds altogether. Blend the cornflour into the juice and stir in half the sugar. Heat gently. Separate the eggs. Beat the yolks and pour them over the heated fruit juice. Beat until cool. Whisk the egg whites with the rest of the sugar until stiff and lightly fold into the yolk mixture. Divide amongst four buttered ramekins. Place in a roasting tin containing a little water and bake in the oven for 12–15 minutes at 190°C/375°F/gas mark 5. Serve immediately.

Peaches in honey and lime
SERVES 4

Prepare the syrup the day before required.

2 tablespoons water	1 fresh lime
1 tablespoon clear honey	4 peaches

Heat the water and honey. Grate in the lime zest and squeeze in the lime juice. Bring to the boil. Remove from the heat and allow to stand overnight. Next day, peel and stone the peaches and pour on the syrup. Chill for an hour or so before serving.

Pomegranate sorbet
SERVES 2
GENEROUSLY

This is a very delicate sorbet; the flavour is scarcely present, but unmistakable. Not a sorbet to serve as part of a *grand dessert*. Fortunately the pomegranate season coincides with the only time of year when we can get fresh imported purple figs at a decent price. The two go together marvellously since neither has an overpowering flavour, but the textures and temperatures couldn't be more different. A spoonful of pomegranate sorbet, then a bite of a luscious fig. Quite blissful.

The sorbet has no sugar in it so should be served as soon as it's ready. If you leave it in the freezer it will set rock hard in no time.

4 pomegranates	¼ pint/150 ml water and fresh
1 teaspoon gelatine crystals	orange juice, mixed

Cut the pomegranates in half and squeeze out all the juice. I find a lemon squeezer perfect for this. Strain the juice into a jug. Sprinkle the gelatine crystals on half the liquid and let it soften for 5 minutes. Heat the rest of the liquid and stir in the gelatine mixture until dissolved. Add to the pomegranate juice and freeze. If you are doing this in a box in the freezer you will need to stir up the crystals from time to time, from the sides to the middle.

Redcurrant kissel
SERVES 4–6

A delicate, light preparation for soft summer fruit. I like to use cherries, raspberries, blackcurrants or redcurrants. This can also be made with any soft autumn fruit – blackberries, bilberries or cranberries. A mixture of all three would also be good.

8 oz/225 g berries	2 tablespoons potato flour
2 oz/50 g sugar – more or less, according to taste	

Pick over the berries. Wash in hot water, drain and crush in a pan with the back of a wooden spoon or a potato masher. Add $\frac{1}{4}$ pint/ 150 ml cold water and rub through a sieve. Boil the residue (skins and seeds) in $\frac{3}{4}$ pint/400 ml of water for 5 minutes then strain. Add the sugar to the water, bring to the boil and stir in the potato flour, previously dissolved in a little cold water. Stir continuously, bring back to the boil, add the first lot of berry juice, mix thoroughly and pour into a glass bowl. Chill and serve when cold and set.

It is important not to boil the mixture for more than 2 minutes or it will begin to thin down again.

Rose and almond jelly
SERVES 6–8

I love to use flowers in cookery, for flavouring and not just for garnish; it is such a thrill to the senses when something tastes exactly as it smells. This jelly is fragrant smelling and rose tasting, and would provide the perfect ending to a summer dinner party. I have a friend who gives me Albertine roses in late May, early June and I find these ideal for such dishes. Begin preparation at least a day before required.

6 oz/150 g almonds
$1\frac{1}{4}$ pints/750 ml water
Petals of 8 fragrant roses in
    full bloom

2 oz/50 g unrefined,
    granulated sugar
5 sheets gelatine or 5
    teaspoons powdered gelatine

Use the freshest almonds you can find, as these will give the most, and the most flavoursome, milk. Blanch them in boiling water to remove the skins. Pound them to a powder using a pestle and mortar if possible. A grinder is not a very good idea as it tends to get clogged up. Put the ground almonds in a basin. Bring $\frac{1}{2}$ pint/300 ml water to the boil and pour this over the almonds. Allow to stand overnight. At the same time, prepare the rose extract. Remove all the rose petals and shake them free of stamens, pollen and tiny beasts. If possible do not wash them, but if you have to, then dry them very carefully so as not to bruise them too much. Put half the petals in an airtight box and put in the refrigerator. Slowly melt the sugar in $\frac{1}{2}$ pint/300 ml water and make it into a syrup, reducing it slightly. When boiling, stir in the rest of the rose petals, allow to boil for 1 minute and remove from the heat. The almonds and roses should stand, covered, overnight to infuse.

Next day melt the gelatine in the remaining ¼ pint/150 ml water and put it into the blender goblet. Strain the rose extract into it, pressing as much liquid as possible from the rose petals. Remove the rest of the petals from the fridge and add these to the blender. Finally, strain the almond 'milk' into it, pressing as much liquid as possible from the ground almonds. Blend until smooth and pinkly milky. Pour into a lightly oiled or wetted 1 lb/450 g loaf tin and refrigerate until set. To serve, turn out on to a plate and slice. Serve one slice each on a pretty dessert plate, with a little thin cream perhaps, or wild strawberries and garnished with a few rose petals.

Allow the ground almonds to dry and use them in a cake or pastry.

Strawberry and orange salad
SERVES 4

A quick, simple summer sweet that will benefit immeasurably from being served on very chilled plates, if you have the time. Far better to chill the plates before dinner than leave the fruit sitting, prepared, in the refrigerator throughout dinner.

4 oranges
½ lb/225 g strawberries
4 tablespoons orangeflower
   water

Black pepper

Grate the zest from the oranges into a small jug. Peel and slice each orange into 5 or 6 slices. Hull and wipe the strawberries. Stir the orangeflower water in the jug with the orange zest. Arrange the orange slices on chilled individual serving plates, and the strawberries on top, sliced or whole, whichever you think looks best. Sprinkle the liquid on top and finish with the lightest sprinkling of freshly and very finely ground black pepper.

Terrine of summer fruits
SERVES 6–8

½ lb/225 g cottage cheese or
   fromage frais
2 oz/50 g unrefined,
   granulated sugar
1 vanilla pod
⅓ pt/200 ml water
2 leaves or 2 teaspoons
   gelatine

2 egg whites
4 oz/100 g raspberries
4 oz/100 g small strawberries
Mint leaves and fruit for
   garnish

Sieve the cottage cheese into a basin. Put the sugar, vanilla pod and most of the water in a saucepan. Melt the sugar and cook gently for half an hour. Meanwhile soak the gelatine in the rest of the water and dissolve it by heating gently. Strain the syrup into the gelatine mix, and combine with the sieved cheese until thoroughly blended. Whisk the egg whites and fold this into the sweetened cheese mixture. Pick over and hull the fruit. Stir them into the cheese mixture and pour into a wetted 1 lb/450 g loaf tin. Refrigerate until set. Turn out on to a plate, slice and serve each slice on an individual dessert plate and garnish with mint leaves and fruit.

A winter fruit salad

Although our own fruit in the winter is limited to apples, pears and nuts, we are lucky enough to receive exotic, tropical fruits almost all the year round. I like to take advantage of this in the winter. After all, in the summer we have delicious things from much nearer home; our own soft, red berry fruits, Spanish apricots, Italian peaches, French nectarines.

Pineapples, papayas, mangoes and guavas from further afield can be expensive however, so you might want to choose just one or two items. Occasionally I can get mangoes quite cheaply when they have become very soft. Then I buy one soft one and one firm one. The soft one I turn into a purée and spoon some on each plate, arranging a few strips of firm mango on top. With a garnish of pomegranate seeds and a trickle or two of pomegranate juice, this becomes a very effective and luscious sweet.

Cream cheese hearts
SERVES 4

This can be prepared in individual heart-shaped, pierced moulds if you have them or, for a do-it-yourself version, take small yoghurt pots or one large one and pierce small holes in the base. Line the moulds with damp muslin or cheesecloth. For the sauce use cooked apricots, or soft fruit such as blackberries, raspberries, red or black currants.

5 oz/150 g thick, plain yoghurt	Sugar or honey to taste
4 oz/125 g curd cheese or sieved cottage cheese	3 egg whites
	12 oz/350 g lightly cooked fruit

Blend the yoghurt and curd cheese until thick and smooth. Whisk the egg whites to firm peaks and fold into the cream, sweetened to taste if you wish. Spoon the mixture into the lined mould(s), place on a tray or dish and refrigerate or stand in a larder for 6–12 hours or overnight to drain.

Make a purée of the fruit by rubbing it through a sieve and spoon it on to a serving dish or individual dessert plates. Turn the cream cheese out, by now light and firm, on top of the sauce.

English lavender pudding
SERVES 6–8

For this you need lavender sugar, which is stocked by some grocers and delicatessens with a range of French imports. Why it is not made in England, where we have such lovely lavender, I do not know. I certainly make my own every year from lavender that is just coming into flower, but not fully in bloom. I pick off the individual flower heads with tweezers – yes, a tedious job indeed – allow them to dry for half a day, and then put them in a well-cleaned coffee grinder with five times their volume of unrefined granulated sugar and grind to a powder, which I allow to dry on a plate and then store in airtight jars. Rose petal sugar and mint sugar I prepare in just the same way. If you can use fresh lavender in this recipe to infuse in the cream, so much the better for you will get the lavender flavour without having to use as much sugar.

1 dessertspoon fruit jelly or honey
8–10 thin slices of lightly buttered wholemeal bread
1 pint/600 ml single cream

Lavender sugar to taste
3 size-3 eggs
1 oz/25 g ratafias, macaroons or Amaretti

Spoon the jelly or honey into a 2 pint/1 litre pudding basin. Cut the crusts from the slices of bread and cut each slice into two wedge shaped pieces. Line the basin with the pieces of bread, butter side to basin, overlapping them slightly. Cut a small round of bread to fit the base. Gently heat the cream and stir in the sugar to taste. Remove the cream from the heat and beat in the eggs one by one. Place the ratafia biscuits in the lined basin, cover with any extra bread. Pour the custard through a sieve over the ratafias and bread. Allow to stand for 20 minutes. Tie on a cover of greaseproof paper and steam for one hour. Remove from the pan and allow the pudding to shrink slightly. Turn out on to a plate and decorate as you wish, perhaps with a mixture of fresh and crystallised flower petals. Serve with a little more custard or a fruit *coulis*.

A variation on the theme of the popular summer pudding. Use apricots, apples, prunes, pears, peaches.

Autumn pudding
SERVES 6

½ lb / 225 g mixed, dried fruit
1 pint / 600 ml water, tea or fruit juice

10–12 slices crustless wholemeal bread

Gently poach the dried fruit in the liquid until soft. Add more liquid if the fruit seems particularly dry. You should have about 6–7 fl oz / 200 ml liquid with the cooked fruit.

Line a 2 pint / 1 litre pudding basin with the slices of bread, leaving enough for a lid. Pack the fruit in to the basin and pour on the juice. Cover with more slices of bread cut to fit, cover with a saucer and then weight down. Leave overnight. Turn out on to a pretty serving plate and serve with thin cream or yoghurt.

This is an enormously versatile recipe. The flavouring and garnish can be changed according to season and occasion. Ground coffee and Tia Maria would make a more sophisticated (and less healthy) version. A delicate flavouring of rosewater in the syrup could be enhanced by crystallised rose petals on top and fresh rose petals minced and added to the yoghurt filling. A rum-soaked cake filled with bananas would be rich, alcoholic and toothsome.

Hazelnut sponge
SERVES 6–8

This mixture would also adapt to a Swiss roll recipe, but if you do bake a shallow, flat sponge to roll up, *don't* scatter bran on the baking sheet first. The crunchy crust produced would make it very difficult to roll up the sponge.

3 oz / 75 g wholemeal flour
2 size-3 eggs
3 size-3 egg whites
1 oz / 25 g sugar
2 oz / 50 g ground hazelnuts
1 scant teaspoon baking powder

Filling and garnish
7½ oz / 250 g thick Greek yoghurt
2 oz / 50 g hazelnuts

Syrup
1 dessertspoon honey
Juice of 1 orange
Juice of ½ lemon

First prepare two 8 in/20 cm cake tins. Cut two circles of baking parchment and four 12 in/30 cm strips. Fit two strips in the bottom of each tin, in a cross. Lay the circles of parchment over them. Lightly oil the sides of the tins and the parchment.

Sieve the flour into a basin through a not very fine sieve. This will leave only the coarsest bran behind. But it will not be wasted. Sprinkle it evenly over the baking parchment. As the sponge bakes, a lovely crust will form, and because much of the bran has been removed, the flour will be better able to rise.

Crack the eggs into a pudding basin, add the extra whites and stir in the sugar. Whisk until pale, frothy and much increased in volume, over a pan of hot water. Remove from the heat and continue whisking; about 5 minutes over the heat, and 5 minutes off the heat is about right. Sieve the baking powder into the flour and fold this carefully into the egg and sugar mixture. Then fold in the ground hazelnuts. Divide between the two cake tins and bake towards the top of the oven, pre-heated to 200°C/400°F/gas mark 6 for 12–15 minutes. Meanwhile prepare the filling and the syrup. Stir the yoghurt until smooth. Reserve a few whole hazelnuts for garnish and crush the rest; putting them in a paper bag and crushing with a rolling-pin is the easiest method I know. Heat the honey gently and add the orange and lemon juice.

Remove the cake tins from the oven and allow the sponges to rest for a minute. Ease away from the side of the tin with your fingers or a knife. Using the strips of paper to help you, remove the sponges from the tin and allow to cool on a wire rack, peeling off the baking parchment first.

For a simple gâteau, place one of the sponges on a plate, sprinkle with a little syrup and spread the yoghurt on quite thickly. Place the second sponge on top. Brush more syrup over the surface, covering it completely, but reserving a tablespoon or so in the pan. Boil this up until sticky and brush on a 1 in/2.5 cm border of syrup around the edge of the cake. Sprinkle on a border of crushed hazelnuts and garnish with whole nuts. For a more elaborate-looking cake, slice each sponge into two circles, giving you three layers of filling.

Because it is moist, this cake keeps very well until the next day. Unlike cream, the yoghurt remains very fresh-tasting and white.

Mincemeat is not itself particularly 'healthy' but at least if you make it yourself you can control the amount of sugar and fat that goes into it. Here are a couple of dishes which can be served during the various Christmas feasts. Since one of their main ingredients is air, they will at least feel light.

Petits clafoutis de Noël
MAKES 12

1 portion of *clafoutis* batter (see p. 133)
3 oz/75 g mincemeat

Using a non-stick bun tin, spoon a little mincemeat into each mould. Pour on the batter and bake in a pre-heated oven, 200°C/400°F/gas mark 6 for 30 minutes. These should be sweet enough, but if you fear they may not be, you could stir a little clear honey into the batter or a little unrefined sugar into the mincemeat.

4 size-3 eggs	Nutmeg or cinnamon	
4 teaspoons mincemeat		
1 tablespoon wholemeal breadcrumbs		

Petits soufflés de Noël
MAKES 4

Separate the eggs. Beat the mincemeat into the egg yolks. Whisk the egg whites until stiff and lightly fold into the yolk mixture. Add the breadcrumbs. Lightly butter 4 ramekins and divide the mixture amongst them. Sprinkle with spices. Bake in a *bain-marie* in the middle of a hot oven, 220°C/425°F/gas mark 7, for 10–12 minutes.

A rich, sticky sweet to serve in small quantities. Follow the instructions for making the paper parcels in the baked apricots recipe on p. 122 but cut smaller shapes, to take 3 prunes. Soak the prunes the day before required.

Prunes in a paper bag
SERVES 6

18 prunes	3–4 oz/75–100 g marzipan or almond paste
1 pot of hot, fragrant tea	½ oz/15 g melted butter
9 walnut halves	

Put the prunes in a basin. Strain the tea over them and let them steep overnight. When plumped out, remove from the tea and dry them. Remove the stone. Cut each walnut half in half again. Break the almond paste into 18 small pieces and mould each one around the walnut. Stuff the prunes with this. Brush melted butter on the paper hearts and place 3 stuffed prunes on each. Moisten with a little tea. Seal each parcel as described on p. 138 and bake in a hot oven, 200°C/400°F/gas mark 6, for 10 minutes. If you wish you could make a syrup by adding sugar to the tea and boiling it until syrupy, to serve with the prunes, but this is rather gilding the lily, I feel.

White chocolate delights
SERVES 4–6

Toffee cake was a favourite sweet in my childhood – a layer of shortbread, toffee made from condensed milk on top of that, and finished with a layer of chocolate. This is a grander version using white chocolate. The cake-part I have experimented with, reducing the sugar content, using wholemeal flour, and sunflower margarine instead of butter, without any loss of flavour.

4 oz/100 g sunflower margarine
1 teaspoon sweet orange oil
Pinch of salt
2 oz/50 g unrefined, granulated sugar
1 egg yolk

6 oz wholemeal self-raising flour
3 or 4 small (1 oz/25 g) white chocolate bars
2–3 oz/50–75 g blanched almonds

Cream the margarine until soft. Beat in the orange oil, salt and sugar. Add the egg yolk and beat well. Gradually add the flour and beat until smooth. Spoon the mixture into a lightly buttered cake tin, round or square, and spread the firmish mixture into a smooth layer. Covering it with clingfilm and smoothing it with your fingers is very effective. Bake for about 20–25 minutes in a pre-heated oven at 180°C/350°F/gas mark 4.

Meanwhile chop the almonds into small pieces or use flaked almonds. Unwrap the chocolate bars. Remove the cake from the oven and lay the chocolate on top, keeping a ¼ in/½ cm border all round. After a minute or two the heat of the cake will begin to melt the chocolate and you can then spread it with a knife or back of a spoon dipped in hot water. Sprinkle the almonds on while the chocolate is still soft and press them well in. Slide a spatula round the sides of the cake to ease it away from the tin, but allow it to cool in the tin. When cool, refrigerate for 10 minutes or so until the chocolate has set. With a sharp knife cut into squares or wedges.

This is a rich, sweet treat for those who love white chocolate. One each at the end of a delicious meal is hardly going to cause much damage. Serve in pretty paper cases, either with other *petits fours* or alone.

White chocolate truffles
MAKES 2

The first time I made these truffles I had also been doing things with kumquats and had made a thick syrup, some crystallised peel and some powdered, flavoured sugar. I put a little syrup inside each truffle, filled the hole with more white chocolate mix and then rolled in flavoured sugar. The kumquat flavour goes perfectly with white chocolate.

1 oz/25 g white chocolate
1 walnut-size piece of unsalted
   butter
1 dessertspoon double cream
Powdered sugar or cocoa

In a small, non-stick saucepan gently melt and stir together the first three ingredients. Allow to cool and then put in the refrigerator or on ice cubes to make quite firm. Then, working quickly, divide the mixture into two, shape into two balls and roll in powdered sugar or cocoa. Chill until firm again and serve.

Cooking methods

In this chapter I thought it would be useful to describe some of the more unusual methods of cooking and preparing food, methods which produce a healthy and tasty end result in that the food is cooked or prepared retaining its full flavour and texture. Raw food obviously requires no 'method', but it is an important element in food preparation, an element which I try to include in as many meals as possible in one form or another, whether it is a salad, fresh fruit or a raw fish appetiser.

DRY FRYING

This is probably the method I most often use for cooking meat since it is economical, not requiring the oven and practical, particularly in cooking for two. Since we tend to eat few joints of meat, it is a method I use, say, for lamb steaks or chicken breasts, and certainly for fish cutlets. I use non-stick frying pans, but a well-seasoned cast-iron frying pan is also excellent for this method of cooking. This is all the equipment you need. Have your fish or meat ready to hand. Heat the pan until almost smoking if cooking meat, to a lower temperature for fish, place the food in the pan, seal it on one side and then lower the heat to cook it a little. Raise the heat again and turn the food over to seal the other side. Cook until it is done as you like it and remove from the pan to a warm place. Here is the bit I like best, making the sauce. Get the pan hot again and pour on stock. This you then boil and bubble fiercely until much reduced, by which time the texture will have changed to a recognisable, suave, velvety sauce. Season and serve with your fish or meat.

With practice, and a large enough frying pan, you can prepare the main course in the middle of a dinner party.

COOKING IN A BAG

Normally used for roasting the traditional joint, hence their trade name, these tough versatile bags (which look like ordinary plastic bags) are useful for cooking many dishes where you want to retain the cooking juices and also afford some protection from direct heat. That they provide a clean and easy method of cooking is, for me, an added bonus, not the main reason I use them.

Whole fish such as mackerel, 'joints' of fish such as a monkfish tail, small pieces of meat such as a saddle of hare, a fillet of beef, a tender young leg of lamb, all cook to perfection when placed in a bag, together with appropriate seasoning, and baked in the oven.

If you are cooking meat, or indeed anything which has a fair amount of fat in it, you should sprinkle a teaspoon of flour into the bag before putting in whatever it is to be cooked. Chestnut flour, potato flour or wholemeal can be used, as well as white flour. Chestnut flour combines particularly well with the cooking juices from, say, a fillet of beef or venison to produce an exceedingly tasty gravy.

It is important to remember to make a few slits in the top of the bag to let the steam escape, otherwise your dish will not roast properly. It is equally important that there is plenty of room in the bag and that it is loosely tied. The bag should not be placed directly on the oven shelf but in a roasting tin or on a baking sheet, and you should make sure that it doesn't touch any part of the oven. Liquid, be it wine, water, stock, melted butter or oil, can also be added to the bag with the main ingredient to provide yet more gravy.

Roasting is not the only way of using these bags. I have cooked a small ham in one in a pan of simmering water to good effect. A boned and stuffed saddle of rabbit was particularly successful cooked this way, because the stuffing didn't drift off as it might have done had I poached it. Vegetables placed in a bag and cooked in a large pan of boiling water retain all their vitamins and so much flavour that you will not even want to serve them with melted butter.

COOKING IN A PARCEL

Paper bag cookery, called *en papillote* or *al cartoccio* on smart menus, is fun, healthy and easy to do. I like to serve food to guests this way for it's a little dramatic and suspenseful as each individual parcel is opened on the dinner plate. And there is really no end to what can be cooked this way; cutlets of salmon, fillets of sea bass, chicken, fruit, even spaghetti *al cartoccio*. On the other hand, I think there are shapes of food that lend themselves to this preparation and shapes that don't. Chicken breasts can be folded into a neat parcel; a whole chicken, even a small one, can not. Anything with bones, sharp points or angles that might pierce the paper is unsuitable, so pieces of fish rather than the whole fish, fillets of lamb rather than a joint, breast of pheasant rather than the whole bird are what you should use. Scallops and other shellfish are, of course, excellent.

As with roasting bags, this is a way of cooking food in its own juices, so that you will feel less inclined to smother the flavours with butter, cream and sauces. However, the paper is not as strong a wrapping as the roasting bag, and care must be taken not to char the parcel. A medium hot rather than a very hot oven is best, and not too long a cooking time, even for the sturdiest greaseproof paper or baking parchment which you will use to wrap the food. The paper should be cut to provide ample room for the food as well as a generous edge to fold over and seal. Traditionally, a heart shape is cut from a folded sheet of paper. Like many traditions it is based on good sense as this shape, folded over, can be sealed quite easily by rolling and tightly folding together the two edges. If you wish, you can brush the paper with stock, oil, melted butter, honey, syrup, depending on what you are planning to cook in the parcel. Seasoning should also be added with the main ingredient before the paper is sealed up. The parcels should then be placed on a baking sheet and put into the top half of the oven.

CLAY POT COOKING

This is yet another method of cooking ingredients in the oven in a closed container in such a way as to require no added fat or liquid. These large, lidded pots are made of earthenware, sometimes glazed inside, sometimes not. To me they are rather clumsy and rustic, and I like to cook simple casseroles or soups which require long slow cooking and which I can bring to table in the clay pot. Dried beans are marvellous cooked in this way, particularly when you add a small piece of pork or bacon. Casseroles or root vegetables, flavoured with herbs and spices, are also excellent.

Some pots come with instructions which I found I needed to adapt. Whilst I can see the sense of soaking the porous clay pot in fresh cold water for 10–15 minutes before use, in order to provide the moisture for cooking, I do not see the point of cooking it for a long time in a hot oven. This simply overcooks the food and seems not at all necessary. It can be put into a cold oven, however, which makes clay pot cooking ideal for those who like their dinner to start cooking while they are out, using an automatic timer.

If you decide that this is a method you like for cooking fish, then you should really invest in a second pot. However carefully you clean it, because it is porous, some cooking smells linger. You will find it a good method for cooking puddings if you like rice puddings, dried fruit compotes and baked apples. And so a third pot may be necessary. As I have little storage space, I use my single pot for casseroles and winter soups and push it to the back of an inconvenient cupboard for the summer months.

POACHING

This is the method I like best of all for cooking food I want to serve cold.

The only equipment you need is a container large enough to hold whatever it is you want to cook and enough water to cover it. This might be a fish kettle, if you are lucky enough to have one, or even luckier to have a fishmonger who will lend you one, or simply a large saucepan or jam pan.

The poaching liquid will depend on what you are cooking. Fish can be poached in water, a mixture of water and wine, milk and water (particularly good for smoked haddock), stock. Chicken can be poached in stock or a herb-flavoured mixture of water and wine. Fruit such as peaches, plums or apricots can be poached in apple juice with honey and spices, other fruit juices, wine, or what you will. The liquid which is left after poaching the food, whether savoury or sweet, can be the base of your accompanying sauce, or if a stock, a marvellous soup for another day. If you plan to use the stock for sauce, do not salt it at the beginning, since you will need to reduce it considerably, and this would make a salted stock into an inedibly salty sauce.

To poach a whole fish

Wrap the cleaned, gutted and prepared fish loosely in muslin, or slip a few double-thickness strips of foil under it so that you can lift it out of the container without breaking it. Place the fish in a suitably sized container and cover it with water. Add parsley stalks, a few peppercorns, one or two slices of peeled onion, a leafy piece of celery and a piece of lemon or orange zest. Put this on to a moderate heat and bring the liquid slowly to the boil. When it boils, allow it to simmer gently (i.e. with scarcely any breaking of the water's surface) for 3 minutes, then remove from the heat and allow the fish to cool in the liquid. It will naturally continue to cook in the hot liquid beyond the 3 minutes, simmering and you will find that it will be perfectly cooked, yet still moist, when cold.

If you want to serve the fish hot, you will need to let it simmer, once it comes to the boil, for approximately 8 minutes per pound.

To poach a chicken

I believe this method is an oriental one but I am not sure where I first came across it. It works on the same principle as cooking jacket potatoes on spikes in the oven. The metal spike conducts heat evenly through the potato and it thus cooks from the inside as well. Take a cleaned and prepared chicken and stick about four metal skewers into it, making sure that they go through the thickest part, i.e. the thighs and body, as well as the breast. Place the chicken in a large pot or saucepan. Cover with water. Add a peeled chopped carrot, a sliced celery stalk, a chopped onion, with at least the inner layer of brown skin which will give a good colour to the stock, a chopped leek if you have it, parsley stalks, some sprigs of tarragon if you can, and a few peppercorns. Bring slowly to the boil and barely simmer for 10 minutes. Remove from the heat and let the chicken go cold in the stock.

STEAMING

Cooking food by steaming is a technique which cooks in England have had in common with cooks in North Africa, in France and in China for a very long time. But how varied the finished products are – a *couscous* is so different from a basket of steamed scallops and ginger, a Christmas pudding so different from a salmon steamed with seaweed. But the quality of the basic ingredient is something that all these cuisines have in common.

Steaming is a very plain method of cooking, giving you an unadorned, simple dish as your end product. So your fish, your meat, your vegetables, whatever you are cooking, have got to be impeccable – fresh, firm, sweet-smelling and unblemished.

It is also a very healthy method of cooking, preserving the colour, texture and flavour of whatever you are steaming. It is a method which adds no calories, so you will not want to mask your finished dish with a rich sauce; another reason for using the best quality ingredients you can afford. This is not to say that it is a method of cooking that requires expensive ingredients. What I am suggesting is that if you are steaming courgettes (for example), you want the best looking, smallest, firmest courgettes that you can find, not the limp, blemished specimens with which we are so often palmed off by greengrocers.

People fear sometimes that such a method of cooking requires much intricate equipment. It doesn't *require* it, although I must admit it is fun to have specific pans for certain tasks – I'd love a *couscousière* or a set of bamboo steamer baskets of the kind that hold *dim sum* in the best Cantonese restaurants. But I find that you can do an awful lot with a simple metal steamer basket or two, and a folded tea-towel. One of the most exquisite steamed dishes I have ever tasted was cooked for me by my Chinese sister-in-law who took a large saucepan, put in two to three inches of water, placed in that an upturned pudding basin on which she set a shallow soup plate containing a trout curled round on itself. She sprinkled the fish with a drop of dry sherry and soy sauce, put the lid tightly on the pan, brought the water to the boil and steamed it for 10 minutes or so. A moist, succulent fish cooked with minimal equipment, by a method that I have often used since.

So it is not an expensive way of cooking. If you plan your meal carefully, you can cook the whole thing on one ring, as in the recipes on pp. 85–86. One-pot cooking of this order is ideal for camping or self-catering holidays of course.

Very elegant dishes can be produced by steaming and it is a technique much used in the newer styles of cooking, *cuisine minceur* in the early '70s and now *cuisine naturelle*.

It can be exciting too, when you use different ingredients to scent the steam. Fish cooked with seaweed is a classic, from which I developed my recipe using samphire. Herb-scented steam adds a delicate flavour which, if well chosen, will complement your main ingredient rather than fight it. I love cooking with scented flowers, using them not so much as decoration but as a flavouring, particularly lavender and other plants containing fragrant oils.

MARINATING

This is not a cooking technique but a method of preparing food I sometimes like to use.

To marinate or to macerate? Let's dispose of that confusion at the outset. My understanding of the maceration technique in cooking is that it is a process whereby food is soaked in a liquid, either for the purposes of softening it or flavouring it or both. Once the required point of flavouring or softening has been reached, the food is then served, without undergoing any further cooking process. Thus, raw fish or dried fruits are macerated and served with or without the liquid in which they were soaked.

To marinate an ingredient is to place it in a bath of liquid with or without herbs, flavourings and other seasonings. The purpose is to change its texture perhaps, by tenderising it, to add to its flavour with herbs or garlic, or to otherwise improve it before it is finally cooked. And here the marinade is often cooked with the ingredient, at some stage, to provide the sauce. Thus you might marinate a piece of game in some red wine with herbs and garlic for a day or two, then cook it adding the strained marinade as the cooking liquor.

Long gone are the days, I hope, when careful cooks would try to disguise dubious meats in highly spiced and alcoholic marinades. Nor does it work if you use up your plonk on a good cut of meat. If you use cheap, thin wine you will finish up with a cheap, thin sauce. I shall never forget the occasion when I presented a dish to three cookery competition judges – a casserole of pigeons with walnuts and wild mushrooms. We were only allowed to use one particular brand of red wine in the cooking, which I duly did, reducing it lovingly and adding all kinds of goodies. Said one discerning judge after tasting my creation, 'How interesting! You've used wine vinegar in the sauce', to the embarrassment of the PR people and the senior organising judge, and to my great chagrin. Still it was a lesson worth learning. If I use wine as a marinade, I will only use something that I consider good enough to drink, even if that sometimes leads me into minor extravagances.

Wine is, of course, one of the most usual ingredients for a marinade, either red or white. But you can use a simple mixture of olive oil with lemon juice and herbs; this is very good with fish.

A warm marinade in which you have first brought some root vegetables to the boil imparts the flavour not only of the liquid used but also that of the vegetables.

Spirits are not my favourite marinating ingredients. They are too powerful and alter the texture of food too much for my liking. However I have begun to experiment with the fruit oils, fruit and herb vinegars and fruit juices.

What sort of ingredients marinate well? Game, yes. It is said to be particularly suitable for removing the fishy taste from feathered game such as wild duck, but quite honestly I have never found this a problem. On the other hand, most of the chickens we buy have a distinctly fishy flavour, bearing out the saying that you are what you eat. So unless I am lucky enough to find a free-range well-fed chicken, I marinate chicken. But I hesitate to marinate fish. Almost any wine marinade will change its texture, as will such things as lemon or lime juice. And I prefer to eat it completely raw in most cases – turbot, sole and scallops for example are much nicer raw than marinated. Some of the oilier fish, however, salmon and mackerel, or the firm ones, like monkfish, will take a more robust treatment.

Fruit and vegetables lend themselves to marinades and macerations but beware. Rumpot, the soft fruit layered in a jar throughout the summer and topped up with rum, to be ready in time for Christmas can be dangerously alcoholic.

But used judiciously, marinating is an interesting technique and if you match your marinading liquid to the ingredient, you can obtain delicious and unusual results.

RAW FOOD

I find it's all too tempting in the autumn and winter to throw off the good eating habits acquired during the summer. My mind turns to rich warming food: delicious *cassoulets* and *ragoûts* and slowly simmered casseroles. We all feel some innate need, I suppose, to stoke up, to take fuel on board for the hard winter ahead. It is an urge to be resisted if possible. Our houses and places of work are, for the most part, heated in one way or another, so we do not need fuel food to warm us to the same extent as did our ancestors. On the whole we lead more sedentary lives. A lumberjack might well need to consume the sort of food described above all the time. For most of us it should be the exception rather than the rule; how otherwise shall we use up all the excess energy created?

So, as far as possible, I try to keep to the healthier eating patterns established during the summer, particularly in the amount of raw food eaten. Remember all those crisp green salads and endless platters of fruit? They can just as well form part of an autumn or winter meal providing a sharp, crisp contrast in texture, flavour and colour to the cooked dishes which follow.

Raw food is indeed delicious. It must be of good quality – fresh, ripe, unblemished. You may need more time to select the best. To preserve the essential nutrients, it is as well to handle the fruit or vegetables as little as possible. Prepare them at the last minute. Scrub rather than peel if you can, since much of the vitamin C content is directly beneath the skin. Don't leave them soaking in water. Again, all the goodness drains out. Choose contrasting colours for effect on the plate, dress with a small quantity of tasty dressing, or fruit juice or good oil, and use your best tableware to display these delicious raw treats, so full of fibre and vitamins.

Fruit and vegetables are not the only things which are delicious raw. Thinly sliced fish such as sole, monkfish, mackerel are part of the healthy Japanese diet in the form of *sashimi*. I often serve a raw fish salad dressed with a little oil and vinegar, or a *tartare* of salmon or salmon trout. Steak tartare is a delicious way of eating beef if you like it, but my favourite way of eating raw meat is Italian style. Beef *carpaccio* is very thin slices of raw steak, preferably fillet, pounded even thinner. The slices are laid on a dinner plate and dressed with the finest olive oil. Thin shavings of Parmesan are scattered on top, and then a substantial garnish of something raw and green. I have had *carpaccio* served with finely sliced baby artichokes, celery and *arugola* (rocket), the latter giving a delicious sharp peppery bite to the dish. As with any raw food you serve, you must be absolutely certain that the ingredients are fresh.

Index